Colossians

T&T CLARK STUDY GUIDES TO THE NEW TESTAMENT

Series Editor

Tat-siong Benny Liew, College of the Holy Cross, USA

Other titles in the series include:

1&2 Thessalonians: An Introduction and Study Guide

1 Peter: An Introduction and Study Guide

2 Corinthians: An Introduction and Study Guide

Colossians: An Introduction and Study Guide

Ephesians: An Introduction and Study Guide

Galatians: An Introduction and Study Guide

James: An Introduction and Study Guide

John: An Introduction and Study Guide

Luke: An Introduction and Study Guide

Mark: An Introduction and Study Guide

Matthew: An Introduction and Study Guide

Philemon: An Introduction and Study Guide

Philippians: An Introduction and Study Guide

Romans: An Introduction and Study Guide

The Letters of Jude and Second Peter: An Introduction and Study Guide

T&T Clark Study Guides to the Old Testament:

1 & 2 Samuel: An Introduction and Study Guide

1 & 2 Kings: An Introduction and Study Guide

Ecclesiastes: An Introduction and Study Guide

Exodus: An Introduction and Study Guide

Ezra-Nehemiah: An Introduction and Study Guide

Hebrews: An Introduction and Study Guide

Leviticus: An Introduction and Study Guide

Jeremiah: An Introduction and Study Guide

Job: An Introduction and Study Guide

Joshua: An Introduction and Study Guide

Psalms: An Introduction and Study Guide

Song of Songs: An Introduction and Study Guide

Numbers: An Introduction and Study Guide

Colossians

An Introduction and Study Guide
Authorship, Rhetoric,
and Code

By

Janice Capel Anderson

t&tclark

LONDON • NEW YORK • OXFORD • NEW DELHI • SYDNEY

T&T CLARK
Bloomsbury Publishing Plc
50 Bedford Square, London, WC1B 3DP, UK
1385 Broadway, New York, NY 10018, USA

BLOOMSBURY, T&T CLARK and the T&T Clark logo are trademarks of
Bloomsbury Publishing Plc

First published in Great Britain 2019

Cover design by clareturner.co.uk

A catalogue record for this book is available from the British Library.

A catalogue record for this book is available from the Library of Congress.

ISBN: PB: 978-0-5676-7464-7
ePDF: 978-0-5676-7463-0
ePUB: 978-0-5676-7465-4

Series: T&T Clark Study Guides to the New Testament, volume 13

Typeset by Newgen KnowledgeWorks Pvt. Ltd., Chennai, India
Printed and bound in Great Britain

To find out more about our authors and books visit www.bloomsbury.com
and sign up for our newsletters.

To my husband and family. In gratitude for all you bring to my life and the lives of others.

Contents

Acknowledgments

I wish to thank my students, who teach me at least as much as I teach them. Thanks are also due to the University of Idaho, my professional home for many years. Finally, I want to acknowledge the kindness and patience of my editor, Tat-siong Benny Liew.

Note on Text and Translation

Many of the translations of the biblical text are my own. Where this is not the case, I have indicated the translation used, largely the New Revised Standard Version.

Abbreviations

ABD	David Noel Freedman (ed.), *The Anchor Bible Dictionary* (New York: Doubleday,1992)
ABRL	Anchor Bible Reference Library
AJEC	Ancient Judaism and Early Christianity
AYB	Anchor Yale Bible
BibSem	The Biblical Seminar
BNTC	Black's New Testament Commentaries
Bull Eng Geol Environ	*Bulletin of Engineering Geology and the Environment*
ECAM	Early Christianity in Asia Minor
EvQ	*Evangelical Quarterly*
HUT	Hermeneutische Untersuchungen zur Theologie
ICC	International Critical Commentary
JBL	*Journal of Biblical Literature*
JETS	*Journal of the Evangelical Theological Society*
JJS	*Journal of Jewish Studies*
JR	*Journal of Religion*
JSNT	*Journal for the Study of the New Testament*
JSNTSup	*Journal for the Study of the New Testament, Supplement Series*
LASLA	Laboratoire d'Analyse Statistique des Langues Anciennes
LNTS	The Library of New Testament Studies

NIB	Keck, Leander E. (ed.) (1994–2004), *The New Interpreter's Bible,* 12 vols. Nashville, TN: Abingdon.
NIGTC	The New International Greek Testament Commentary
NovTSupp	*Novum Testamentum,* Supplements
NPNF	Nicene and Post-Nicene Fathers
NTL	New Testament Library
NTS	*New Testament Studies*
PFES	Publications of the Finnish Exegetical Society
RevExp	*Review and Expositor*
SB	Sources bibliques
SBLDS	SBL Dissertation Series
SBLSS	SBL Semeia Studies
SBLSBS	SBL Sources for Biblical Study
SP	Sacra Pagina
TNTC	Tyndale New Testament Commentaries
WBC	Word Biblical Commentary
WUNT	Wissenschaftliche Untersuchungen zum Neuen Testament

A Word to the Reader

As you begin reading, I want to explain some of the features of this guide and suggest how you might approach it. The guide is written primarily for undergraduate, graduate, and seminary students as well as other readers who want an introduction to the interpretation of Colossians. Each chapter begins with a series of thought experiments or exercises. I hope these will help you to bridge the gap between your own experience and scholarly questions. The goal is to develop some preliminary ideas and skills that will assist you to analyze and evaluate actively. I recommend having a Greek text of Colossians by your side if you read Greek. If not, a physical parallel bible that sets several English translations in parallel columns would be helpful. Or, if you have access to the internet, you can use one of the sites that allow you to compare translations. The Society of Biblical Literature's Bible Odyssey website is one, but there are others. The guide often refers to specific verses, and being able to see the Greek or alternate translations will prove useful. I have sometimes provided my own somewhat literal translations to allow you to see the text before translators have smoothed it and interpreted it. (Of course, I may be doing the same.) One translation note is that I have translated the Greek *Ioudaios* as Jew rather than Judean. I think Jew best captures the complex mixture of ethnic, geographical, and religious identity the term represents. For thought-provoking discussions of the issue, see the *Marginalia* website's 2014 "Jew and Judean: A Forum on Politics and Historiography in the Translation of Ancient Texts" (Law and Halton) and Cynthia M. Baker's 2017 book, *Jew*.

Turning from translation to content, I have focused in this guide on three areas that scholars have pursued, sometimes with an intensity that may surprise you. The first is the question of authorship. The second is the rhetoric of the letter and the identity of people the letter may oppose. The third is a section of Colossians called the household code, which raises ethical questions about marriage relationships, treatment of children, and slavery. I am acutely aware that I have had to pick and choose not only what topics to cover, but also how to cover them in a short guide. If you want more depth and coverage, I highly recommend borrowing from a library several commentaries that have introductory sections and a verse-by-verse detailed commentary. Choose commentaries that reflect different religious, methodological (i.e., literary, social scientific, or theological methods), geographical, and cultural perspectives. I am a university professor, and I try to follow the advice of one of my former colleagues: to teach students to charitably entertain many views including the views of those with whom they disagree. The students then have better grounds for developing their own considered positions and understanding those of others. I often encourage this through small group discussions with students bringing different perspectives to the table. I hope you will have this opportunity as you read this guide. If not, reading multiple commentaries can provide a similar experience. Since the guide inevitably reflects my interests, perspectives, and blind spots, I also suggest you look at a variety of commentaries as a supplement. If you do not need to sell the guide back, I encourage you to write evaluative comments in the margins. You should write comments like "unclear" or "big assumption," but I also hope you will occasionally write "interesting" or "important." Finally, I often use "we" to include readers, and frankly, to avoid passive voice. "As we see" is stronger than "it can be seen that." If you do not see yourself as part of any "we," note that in the margin as well.

Janice Capel Anderson

Stories of Colossians and Authorship

Thought Experiment One—Harry Potter, the Third Generation

Imagine that five years after J. K. Rowling's death, someone discovers a computer printout of a chapter describing Harry Potter's granddaughter's first day at Hogwarts. In it, the Sorting Hat determines the granddaughter to be a Slytherin. The chapter gives J. K. Rowling as the author. There are some differences in vocabulary and style from Rowling's earlier Potter books. It seems odd that the granddaughter wears a "sweater" rather than a "jumper."

That the granddaughter is a Slytherin also seems odd to devotees of the eight Potter books ending with *The Deathly Hallows*. It does not seem out of the realm of possibility, however. In the play, *Harry Potter and the Cursed Child*, written by Jack Thorne (2016), based on a story by Thorne, Rowling, and John Tiffany, Albus Severus Potter, Harry's son, is a Slytherin. The chapter is engaging and makes the reader want to read more. It takes the characters from the earlier books in new, but recognizable directions. The printout comes from a printer that was in use while Rowling was still alive, but many people still use the same printer. To complicate matters, Rowling (let us imagine) was known to create working outlines for her books and to dictate her work to an American secretary as her eyes failed with age.

What are some ways that scholars might try to determine whether Rowling herself, a close friend, a collaborator, or someone unknown to her produced the chapter? For what purposes and in what respects would it make a difference in your view?

For an exercise that raises issues about existing Harry Potter works and the concept of a canon, see Dalton (2017).

Thought Experiment Two—Nancy Drew and the Hardy Boys

The popular Hardy Boys and Nancy Drew book series introduce many children to the joy of reading mysteries. You may be surprised to learn that authors Franklin W. Dixon and Carolyn Keene are pseudonyms for a series of ghostwriters. Does the fact that a single person did not write all the books make a difference? Would you as a reader care if you knew that the earliest Nancy Drew books were written by Mildred Wirt Benson and the later ones by another author? Would you care if you learned that plot outlines for the early books were provided to the ghostwriters? Would you view or read each of the mysteries differently?

For still controversial discussion about the authorship of the Nancy Drew books, see Keleny (2014), Rehak (2005), and Johnson (1993).

Stories of Colossians

There are several accounts or stories that one might tell about Colossians as a letter from its sender to its first recipients. In one story, Paul dictates a letter to the Colossians. His secretary may have been his coworker Timothy, mentioned as a co-sender in the letter's greeting. Paul is a prisoner. He has heard about those who follow Christ in the Lycus River Valley of Roman Asia Minor (Turkey), including the cities of Colossae, Hierapolis, and Laodicea. Paul has learned about the community in Colossae from Epaphras, a member of the community and a fellow slave of Christ now with him. Writing from prison, Paul wants to encourage the Colossians and to counteract what he sees as false teaching and practices among them. Whether the source of the teaching and practices is internal to the community or external is not clear. The alternative "philosophy" involves visions, the worship of or with angels, ascetic restrictions on eating and drinking, and "observing festivals, new moons, or sabbaths" (Col 2:8, 16, New Revised Standard Version [NRSV]). Even though Paul himself did not found the church and cannot be present with them, his spirit is with them. He wants them to know how much he struggles and suffers for them. He wants them to understand the mystery of Christ and how to live on that basis. Paul assumes that they know about him and are in touch with a network of the faithful that is part of the Pauline mission. He sends the letter with Tychicus and Onesimus (also, one of them), who will report to them orally. He ends the letter with greetings from members of his network. He also asks that they extend his greetings to the Christ followers in Laodicea including "Nympha and the assembly in her house" (4:15). The Colossians are to have their letter read to the Laodiceans and they are to read a letter Paul sent to the Laodiceans. Paul closes the letter to the Colossians with a greeting in his own handwriting and asks them to "Remember my chains" (4:18, NRSV).

A second story about the letter to the Colossians involves a fictive author. That is, someone else—whether an individual or a group—composes Colossians as if the author is Paul. The recipients may or may not be residents of Colossae. A particularly poignant form of this story told in slightly different versions by Angela Standhartinger (2004) and Hans Dieter Betz (1995) is that Paul has been martyred. Close companions write a letter that transmits an image of Paul reflecting the presence of Paul and his teaching that they knew when he was alive and may still experience in memory or in prayer. Through the letter read in worship, Paul can speak from heaven. This heavenly letter provides the living presence of Paul for its recipients. Though Paul is absent in the flesh, he is present in the spirit. This function is similar to other letters of Paul, which substitute for the physical presence of Paul and his companions when they are absent. "Paul" writes to encourage the faithful to stand fast in the face of his suffering and death, to remember his chains.

There are, of course, further modifications of these two stories that scholars and others tell. Some hold that Paul and Timothy coauthored the letter. Others that Timothy or Epaphras named in Col 1:7–8 and 4:12–13 wrote to the Colossians on Paul's behalf shortly before or after Paul's death. If before, Paul may have given a general idea of what he wanted to say and signed off in his own handwriting. Still others tell a story of a fictional author or a pseudepigrapher (literally, a false writer) claiming to be the historical Paul with an intent either to deceive or to control how Pauline tradition was to be interpreted and put into practice. This author borrowed Paul's authority to support his or her own views. The references to Paul's chains, specific coworkers, Nympha's house church, and the claim to write the closing in Paul's own hand are touches designed to persuade audiences that the letter is genuine. They are not marks of authenticity as other interpreters maintain. For those who tell a story of fictive authorship—whether of close companions extending Paul's message into the future or of deceit—there are also multiple accounts of how the letter was composed. The author(s) may have used written copies of other Pauline letters, may have heard Pauline letters and borrowed from them, or been steeped in oral traditions about Paul and reflected that influence. The form of the letter with its greeting, thanksgiving, body, ethical exhortation, and closing matches other Pauline letters, whether because this is Paul's own format or due to imitation.

Why so many stories?

These stories of Colossians are fascinating. But why are so many told? One reason is that in all of the New Testament letters attributed to Paul, we never grasp the living flesh of the "real" Paul, a man of the first century, or the real addressees in their complex interactions with Paul, his associates, and one another. As individual readers or as communities of interpreters, we always reconstruct the implied sender(s) and the implied addressees, not living and breathing persons. The ancient commonplace was that a letter substitutes for the presence of its author in his or her absence. Paul's letters often have an impact precisely because their rhetoric gives us a sense of that "presence." If we let that rhetoric impact us, we may find the letter addresses us as much as its original addressees—whether we wish to assent, to resist, or both. It helps to remember that even when we write a letter ourselves, we project a version of ourselves in writing. We imagine our addressees and how they may respond to our words. In Colossians, we find the Paul (and perhaps the Timothy) the letter and its readers construct engaged with implied addressees, also constructed by the letter and its readers. It is not that there was not a "real" author or authors and a "real" original audience or audiences. But, as with all past events, we must reconstruct them and this leads to differing reconstructions and differing stories of Colossians. Among biblical scholars the debate over who authored Colossians and the original addressees and their situation—which story of the letter should be told—has been central to the interpretation of the letter. It has encompassed and in some cases eclipsed discussion of the contents of the letter. In this chapter, we discuss first why some scholars question and yet others affirm that the historical Paul wrote Colossians. Then we turn to ask, for what purposes does nailing down authorship make a difference? Finally, we ask why there is such a passionate commitment to asking and answering the question of authorship.

The authorship debate: Historical background

In Western scholarly circles, a debate about who authored Colossians has taken place at least since the 1838 publication of E. T. Mayerhoff's *Der Brief an die Colosser: Mit vornehmlicher Berücksichtigung der 3 Pastoralbriefe kritisch geprüft*. Mayerhoff thought that Paul did not author Colossians because the letter derived from Ephesians (which he viewed as authentic), it addressed a heresy that did not exist in Paul's lifetime, and there were differences in style, vocabulary, and the meaning of terms from letters Paul actually wrote. The debate over the authorship of Colossians was part of a larger debate about the authorship of letters attributed to Paul. The larger debate gained prominence with F. C. Baur's influential division of the Pauline letters in the New Testament into three categories: undisputed, disputed, and spurious ([1845] 1876, 1:246–47). In effect, Baur, an important German Protestant scholar, set out a Pauline canon within the canon literally echoing the fourth-century early church historian Eusebius's categories for early Christian writings more generally ([1845] 1876, 1:246–47). According to Baur, only Romans, Galatians, and 1 and 2 Corinthians, the so-called principle letters (*Hauptbriefe*), were surely written by Paul. Baur placed Colossians among the disputed letters. He ultimately argued that Colossians and Ephesians, which he treated as very closely related, did not stem from the historical Paul. His main criteria were theological and contextual. He argued that these letters had a late, high Christology (view or doctrine of Christ) unifying opposites such as heaven and earth and embracing the entire universe ([1845] 1875, 2:35–36). They assumed Christ's preexistence. They were also conversant with gnostic ideas and terminology, including, in Baur's view, myths involving reunion with the divine not present during the life of Paul ([1845] 1875, 2:7–21). Further, Colossians addressed Ebionitism (a type of Jewish Christianity that kept some of the law), which he saw as a Jewish Christian heresy present across Asia Minor rather than a local group of opponents ([1845] 1875, 2:28–32). As a practical matter, Baur argued, Colossians and Ephesians were concerned with unifying Gentile and Jewish Christians, a post-Pauline development in his view. They accomplished this by setting faith and works side by side ([1845] 1875, 2:35–40). They abandoned what for Baur was the "authentic" Pauline emphasis on justification by faith "as an inward process in the consciousness, the most essential part of which is a personal conviction and experience of the impossibility of justification through the law" ([1845] 1875, 2:41). This fit into Baur's overall picture of early Christian history. Baur, who was influenced by German philosopher G. W. F. Hegel, held that Jewish Christianity was a thesis, while Gentile Christianity was an antithesis, and a later early Catholicism that rendered them compatible provided a synthesis (Hafemann 1998, 286–89; Krause and Beal 2002, 20–22). In terms of Colossians, Baur also saw a downhill course from the principle letters in terms of style, but less in Colossians than in Ephesians. Of Colossians, he wrote, "in many passages it also gives us the impression of a composition without life or spontaneity, moving forward in repetitions and tautologies, and sentences grouped together with a merely outside connexion" ([1845] 1875, 2:35). All these concerns and more would play out from the nineteenth century on as German scholarship dominated academic biblical studies in the West.

The debate about Pauline authorship in general and of Colossians in particular continues today with some defending and some opposing Pauline authorship. While theologically conservative scholars saw and still see Baur's identification of the *Hauptbriefe* as the only "authentic" letters of Paul as a challenge to faith, what perhaps was not so readily apparent was that the choice of these letters also reflected a German Lutheran understanding of justification by faith and Paul as the apostle of justification. The heart of the gospel and the heart of Paul embodied in his letters matched in ways that liberal Protestants found congenial. Further, in a somewhat ironic point of agreement, both those who favor and oppose Pauline authorship often use the "undisputed" Pauline letters—Baur's *Hauptbriefe* plus in more recent times 1 Thessalonians, Philippians, and Philemon—as the stick against which other letters including Colossians are measured.

Modern views on the authorship of Colossians

As we noted earlier, for Colossians, common suggestions about its authorship include the following: (1) Paul authored the letter alone; (2) Paul and Timothy named as the senders of the letter in 1:1 cowrote the letter; (3) Paul used an amanuensis (a scribe or secretary) who exercised a degree of freedom and influenced the composition; (4) a colleague such as Timothy or Epaphras named in Col 1:7–8 and 4:12–13 wrote the letter on Paul's behalf either shortly before or after Paul's death. If before Paul's death, possibly with Paul commissioning and/or signing off on the letter; and (5) an individual or a group, writing in the name of Paul, composed Colossians after Paul's death, ca. 62–65 C.E. (for Pauline chronology, see Roetzel 1999, 178–83). This selection of alternatives and indeed the whole debate may seem odd at first glance because the first verse names Paul and Timothy as the senders of the letter and the last verse points to Paul closing the letter in his own handwriting: "I, Paul, write this greeting with my own hand. Remember my chains. Grace be with you" (4:18, NRSV). In addition, we have no evidence that early Christians questioned Colossians' Pauline authorship. Colossians appears as a letter of Paul in Marcion's canon, an early list of Paul's letters ca. 110–160 C.E. (Sumney 2008, 12) as well as in $\mathfrak{P}$46, an early papyrus manuscript dated ca. 200–225 C.E. (Pervo 2010, 291 n. 28; Sumney 2008, 12). Neither of these contains the Pastoral Epistles, letters whose authorship scholars also dispute.

So, why do many modern scholars hold that Paul did not compose Colossians? Mayerhoff's and Baur's concerns remain but have been expanded and updated. The arguments that Paul did not compose Colossians fall into three main categories: (1) structure, vocabulary, and style; (2) theology; and (3) social and historical context. The weighting of the evidence in these categories varies. It is also influenced by an initial decision about where the burden of proof lies. Are we to assume that the historical Paul composed Colossians unless a preponderance of evidence suggests otherwise? Or, should we assume that Paul did not compose Colossians unless we have strong evidence that he did? As explained previously, this further depends on establishing a comparison group of letters that the "real" Paul composed. While there are calls to rethink how we establish the historical Paul (Lang 2015; White 2014), currently most scholars accept seven letters as undisputed: Baur's principle letters—Romans, Galatians, and 1 and 2 Corinthians—plus 1 Thessalonians, Philippians, and Philemon. Should the list shift by addition or subtraction, then our notions of Paul's structure, vocabulary, style, theology, and context also shift? Even with the list of the seven undisputed letters as our measure for "Paul," there is no bright line test for how similar the structure, vocabulary, style, theology, and context of a letter must be to count as a letter of the historical Paul. Inevitably, looking for similarities and differences is a matter of a sliding scale. It also involves judgements, as J. C. Beker put it with reference to theology, of coherence and contingency (1984, 11–18). Just how coherent or consistent is Paul across his letters? How much is contingent on the particular situations he addresses?

Nature of authorship

Before we turn to those arguments, however, we must ask, What do we mean by authorship and what might the nature of authorship, particularly of letters, have been in the first century? Typically, in the twenty-first century, when we speak of an author we immediately think of someone sitting at a computer and composing as I am doing now. However, we recognize that authorship can be a more complicated proposition. An editor may suggest changes to a novel, which are made. Coauthors can pass a manuscript back and forth, rewriting as they go. A doctor may dictate patient notes, and a medical transcriptionist enters them in electronic medical records. One family member may compose a holiday letter and present it as from "our family." A senator or a member of Parliament outlines key points she wants to make in a speech. Her speechwriters compose the speech. She makes a few changes, hands it to the teleprompter folks, and delivers the speech. A musician creates a mashup from previous recorded music as DJ Danger Mouse did when he released *The Grey Album*, combining samples from the Beatles' *The White Album* and Jay-Z's *The Black Album* (Wickman 2012).

The authorship of letters in the first-century Mediterranean was complicated in its own way. (See Ehrman 2013, 218–22; Gupta 2013,

209–210; Klauck 2006, chapter two; Murphy-O'Connor 1995, 1–41; Richards 2004; Talbert 2007, 7–11, for a discussion of the process in relation to Paul's letters.) Sometimes authors penned their own missives. At other times, they dictated their letters to a secretary or an amanuensis—either syllable by syllable or by speaking at a normal pace, depending on whether the secretary knew a form of shorthand. An elite person might employ a professional regularly. Others might hire an amanuensis in the marketplace for a single letter. More or less freedom might be given to the secretary in the composition of the letter depending on the circumstances. We know that Paul used a secretary in at least several letters—if not all. In Rom 16:22, the secretary writes, "I, Tertius, the one having written this letter, greet you in the Lord." On several occasions as a form of signature, Paul or someone writing as Paul adds a few words in his own handwriting. In Gal 6:11, we read, for example, "See in what large letters I have written to you in my own hand." Similarly, in Col 4:18a, "This greeting is in my own hand Paul." (See also 1 Cor 16:21, 2 Thess 3:17, and Phlm 1:19.) A further complication is that a number of Pauline letters mention more than one sender. Was this just a courtesy reference to companions or did Paul and his companions discuss or share in the composition? What was the process by which earlier traditions such as baptismal formulas and references to biblical texts were incorporated into the letters? We simply do not know what the procedures were for the production of the Pauline letters. Some scholars explain differences in style and content between the undisputed letters and disputed letters like Colossians as due to the use of secretaries. Others, such as Ehrman, dismiss the "secretary hypothesis" in support of Paul's authorship of disputed letters as "wishful thinking" (2013, 222).

In addition to the vexed question of the process of authorship, the many verbal similarities between Colossians and Ephesians further complicate matters. While the authorship of both letters is disputed, Colossians is more often thought to come from Paul or a close colleague near the time of Paul's death than is Ephesians. Ephesians, many argue, is based on Colossians, authored later by someone in a Pauline "school," a group that preserved and collected Paul's letters as well as writing new letters applying Paul's teachings. Alternatively, some argue that Colossians is a shortened version of Ephesians, an earlier letter authored by Paul. Obviously, there are other possibilities: Paul wrote both the letters, possibly using a secretary; Paul wrote one of the letters and a follower the other; after Paul's death, a follower wrote both the letters; alternatively, two different followers of Paul authored Colossians and Ephesians after his death.

Arguments against and for Paul's authorship of Colossians

Turning again to the main arguments that Paul did not compose Colossians, let us consider (1) structure, vocabulary, and style; (2) theology; and (3) historical context in turn.

Structure, vocabulary, and style

The letter structure of Colossians is very similar to the structure of undisputed Pauline letters. A greeting is followed by a thanksgiving. This, in turn, is followed by the body of the letter with its main arguments and a section of ethical exhortation. It concludes with final, personal greetings. There is nothing about the structure itself that waves red flags. But, what about the letter's vocabulary?

The issue of vocabulary arises both because Colossians contains words that do not occur in the seven undisputed letters and because it lacks some words that appear frequently there. The assumption is that the vocabulary in Colossians should be very similar to the vocabulary in the undisputed letters if Colossians stems from Paul. According to Eduard Lohse, whose commentary on Colossians and Philemon contains one of the most careful discussions of this issue, thirty-four *hapax legomena* (words that appear nowhere else in the New Testament) appear in Colossians ([1968] 1971, 85). An additional twenty-eight words are found elsewhere in the New Testament, but not in the seven undisputed Pauline letters (Lohse [1968] 1971, 85–86, but see Standhartinger 2010, Sect. 2, who puts the count of *hapax legomena* at thirty-four to thirty-seven as well as a total of sixty-one to eighty-seven words that do not occur in undisputed Paulines). This appears impressive until one considers that differing vocabulary may occur simply because of different subject matter. Further, there are thirty-one *hapax legomena* in Galatians (Lohse [1968] 1971, 86–87; O'Brien 1982, xliii) and thirty-nine words in Galatians that occur elsewhere in the New Testament, but in no other Pauline letter (Lohse [1968] 1971, 86–87, n. 146). Yet, no one contests Paul's authorship of Galatians. Similarly, Philippians contains seventy-nine words that do not appear elsewhere in the undisputed Paulines (Brown 1997, 610–611).

In terms of words that occur in the undisputed Paulines but not in Colossians, interpreters are most troubled by the absence of terms such as revelation, righteousness (*dikaiosuné* and related words in Greek), law, and salvation (Lohse [1968] 1971, 86–87; Mayerhoff 1838, 9–27). Here the matter may not be so much vocabulary as theology. These words seem central to Paul's thought to many interpreters. If these words and concepts, however, appear in some contexts but not in others, the context and subject matter may explain their absence. Further, not all these terms appear in all of the undisputed Paulines. For example, salvation (*sótéria*) does not appear in 1 Corinthians or Galatians (Lohse [1968] 1971, 87) and "to justify" does not appear in 1 Thessalonians, Philippians, or 2 Corinthians (Brown 1997, 611). The lack of legal terminology proves surprising to those who see Colossians addressing legalistic opponents (Lohse [1968] 1971, 87) and not at all surprising to those who have a different view of the situation the letter addresses (Barclay [1997] 2004, 29).

At the same time as questions have arisen about unique vocabulary, scholars have also noted some very similar vocabulary and expressions in Colossians and the undisputed Paulines. As Barth and Blanke point out, there are "about fifty of Paul's favorite words, such as the nouns love, brother, truth, apostle, glory, power, peace, church, work, gospel, world, flesh, grace, and the verbs to die, to live, to greet, to admonish" (1994, 58–59).

Oddly enough, in a work that assumes Colossians to be pseudonymous, Outi Leppä (2003), taking her inspiration from a 1966 article by E. P. Sanders, finds many words and phrases from the undisputed letters echoed in Colossians. Rather than treating the echoes as evidence for Pauline authorship, she takes them as evidence for the literary dependence of Colossians on the undisputed letters, although this may include use from memory. She focuses, in particular, on (1) parallels of "more than three similar words (nouns, verbs or adjectives) within five lines in the text imitated" showing "probable literary dependence" and (2) parallels of "at least three similar words (nouns, verbs or adjectives) within five lines in the text imitated" showing "possible literary dependence" (Leppä 2003, 57). Not surprisingly, Sanders (2005) thinks she has made a convincing case for both dependence and authorship by a Pauline disciple. Sumney (2005a) holds that Leppä's criteria for dependence may be too loose, given a lack of exact side-by-side verbal parallels in the same order. Nonetheless, he thinks she has shown the author "was familiar with most of the undisputed Pauline letters, provided one stipulates that Colossians is pseudonymous" (Sumney 2005a, 718). The stipulation is important because as Campbell notes, Paul could have created the echoes and the echoes might result from other letters echoing Colossians (2014, 284–85).

With scholars pointing to both similarities and differences in vocabulary and phrases in favor of and against Pauline authorship, vocabulary does not settle the question of authorship. If vocabulary does not allow us to attribute Colossians to someone other than Paul, are there other elements of style that might?

Among the often-remarked stylistic differences of Colossians from the undisputed Paulines are long sentences strung together with participles, the frequent use of pleonasm (redundancy) including synonyms such as "endurance and patience" in 1:11 and "perfect and filled" in 4:12 and the combination of a verb and noun based on the same root such as "circumcised with a circumcision" in 2:11 as well as chains of genitives such as "the word of truth of the gospel" in 1:5 (Brown 1997, 611; Lohse [1968] 1971, 88–89; O'Brien 1982, xliii; Standhartinger 2010, Sect. 2). Examples of each of these do exist in the undisputed letters, nonetheless. Lohse claimed that these sorts of features marked Colossians' style as more "liturgical-hymnic" than the argumentative style of the major Paulines ([1968] 1971, 89). In 1973 Walter Bujard conducted a study of stylistic features that convinced most German scholars and many others that Paul did not write Colossians (Standhartinger 2010, Sect. 3). Bujard compared the use of various types of conjunctions, percentages of conjunctions, number of infinitives, certain prepositions, repetitions aiming toward a goal, and other features of grammar, syntax, and "rhetorical engagement" in Colossians to those in the seven undisputed Paulines. While on some measures Colossians did not differ from "Paul," on many measures differences stood out. Overall, Bujard argued the evidence demonstrated that the author was not Paul. Among those writing in English, Ehrman (2013, 174–75), Kiley (1986, 51–59), Lincoln (2000, 578), Furnish (1992, 1094), and others find Bujard's statistics convincing. Barclay ([1997] 2004, 30–33) and Campbell (2014, 286–87) find Bujard's data impressive but raise the question of how statistically significant the differences are in marking authorship. Both point in the direction of stylometry or nontraditional authorship attribution employing computer models.

Counting word usage and examining word and sentence lengths are already a form of stylometrics or the statistical measurement of style. Bujard went further. However, it is not clear that the differences he notes are decisive. In recent years, scholars of nontraditional authorship attribution have pursued authorship attribution based on a variety of style markers and statistical methods aided by computer analysis. This has become part of the new field of digital humanities. The puzzle of Pauline authorship has been one arena for this work both by those trained in New Testament studies and by those whose primary interest is computer analysis. Readers may be familiar with Patrick Juola's successful identification via stylometry of J. K. Rowling as highly likely to be the author of the novel *The Cuckoo's Calling* ostensibly by Robert Gailbraith (Juola 2013). A necessary, but unproven, methodological assumption of computer-assisted authorship attribution is that an author's use of language is unique, much like a fingerprint or DNA (Juola 2006b, 239; 2013; Rudman 2012, 265). As a relatively new approach, there are disagreements about what sets of variables in what combinations have a high probability of distinguishing authorship. Variables that lie outside the conscious control of authors such as the use of certain ending letters on words are prized. Scholars also experiment to find the best computational analysis methods for compiling data and analyzing its significance. For those unfamiliar with such work, the overviews of Juola (2006a, 2006b, 2012) and Rudman (2006, 2012) as well as Calle-Martín and Miranda-García's introduction to a 2012 issue of *English Studies* on the topic provide helpful information. They suggest progress is being made, but methods are far from perfect. Some of the most successful forms of analysis have involved comparing a text known to be by one of several authors with texts known to be from each author. In the case of letters attributed to Paul, the issues are more complex.

There have been few sophisticated stylometric analyses of the letters of Paul, and these do not agree with one another on the status of Colossians. The best work so far on Paul is by Kenny (1981, 1986), Ledger (1995), Mealand (1989, 1995), and Neumann (1990)—all of which predate the most recent advances in analysis. This is an area where an enterprising graduate student with skills in New Testament studies and computer science might do some exciting work. However, it also may be that determining a high level of probable authorship by the historical Paul or a single author of a number of the letters labeled as Pauline is hindered by issues that scholars may not be able to resolve. Best practices for stylometry and difficulties are outlined below:

1   Texts to be analyzed via computer should be as close to the original holographs as possible with any editorial material eliminated (Rudman 2006, 613; 2012, 267). With letters ascribed to Paul, this is complicated by the differences between the manuscripts we have of each letter, none of which is close in time to the original holographs.

Further, several of the letters indicate that Paul dictated the letters to scribes and this might be the case for all of them. The letters may have variations introduced by differing scribal hands. Further, we cannot be sure whether Paul dictated syllable by syllable or the scribes used an ancient shorthand. We also do not know whether it was Paul's practice to correct an initial scribal copy before a final version was produced. Beyond that, if one or more of the letters is a product of collaboration between two or more individuals, the problem becomes even more complex.

2 Texts must be stripped of any quotations or foreign language words as well as lemmatized (Rudman 2006, 613; 2012, 267). With Paul, abstracting quotations is problematic. Scholars do not always agree when a passage is a quotation from a source or reflects tradition (oral or written) as well as where the included material begins and ends. The Colossian "hymn" in 1:15–20 is an obvious example as are phrases such as 1 Cor 7:1b (literally "Good for a man not to touch a woman"), which may be a phrase from a letter to Paul or Paul's own view.

3 Studied texts and control texts should be from the same time period such as plus or minus five years and of the same genre (Rudman 2006, 613). If possible, the gender and native language of the authors of texts of any control group of texts should be the same as those of the possible author or authors (Rudman 2006, 613). These elements are designed to eliminate any differences that are not due to individual style. With Paul, the issue of time is particularly important. Scholars sometimes argue that differences between Colossians and the undisputed letters may be due to Colossians having been written late in Paul's life, more than five years after the earliest letters, depending on their chronology. Stylometry has shown that an author's style may change over time (Rudman 2006, 613).

4 The lengths of the texts to be compared should be similar and long enough to reveal an author's style (Holmes 1994, 88). Obviously, the longer the texts for comparison, the better. The Pauline letters, of course, are relatively short. Computer scientists, however, are developing new methods to analyze shorter texts and progress might be made in the future.

The current state of stylometry is not advanced enough to compare as complex a set of materials as the Pauline letters to determine which of them might come from the same author (or authors). In order not to prejudge authorship, analysis would have to place all of the letters attributed to Paul in a set and look for arrays of similarities and differences. Even when stylometry identifies differences and similarities between the Pauline letters, we must interpret their significance (White 2014, 179). If we have no definitive way to determine the authorship of Colossians via computer analyses, can differences in theology make a convincing case?

Theology

More convincing than the analysis of style to some interpreters are aspects of Colossians' theology. Here, too, there are mixed reviews. If we accept the seven undisputed letters as the standard for Paul's theology, how different from the theological aspects of those letters must the theological aspects of Colossians be to point to an author other than Paul? This is complicated by differing assessments of Paul's views in the undisputed letters. It also relies on the assumption that these letters reflect a consistent and coherent theology despite being directed to particular communities, as noted earlier. This, of course, raises the question of how much theological emphases might differ due to addressing a different context or to changes in Paul's thought over time. Further, there is the possibility of coauthorship. The sort of changes some advance as moving a bridge too far are those associated with the systematic theological categories of Christology (views on the nature and function of Christ), eschatology (views on the end of time), ecclesiology (views on the nature of the church), and parenesis (ethics/morality). Let us review each.

Christology

Colossians has what scholars sometimes label a "high" or "cosmic" Christology. This means that Colossians emphasizes Christ's preexistence, cosmic role in creation and redemption, and triumph over opposing forces. It also stresses Christ's nature as the image or icon of God in whom "all the fullness of God was pleased to dwell" (Col 1:19, NRSV). This Christology seems designed to reassure the Colossians of Christ's dominion and complete sufficiency as ruler over all—possibly in the face of claims that baptism into Christ was not sufficient for salvation. As Col 2:9–10 (NRSV) puts it, "For in him the whole fullness of deity dwells bodily, and you have come to fullness in him, who is the head of every ruler and authority." Some scholars argue that such an exalted, cosmic Christology is late and not characteristic of Paul. However, others argue that Colossians reaffirms and extends claims made in the undisputed letters (Sumney 2008, 4–5). First Corinthians 8:6 (NRSV), for example, establishes an exalted role for Christ in creating and sustaining, "yet for us there is one God, the Father, from whom are all things and for whom we exist, and one Lord, Jesus Christ, through whom are all things and through whom we exist." The "hymn" of Phil 2:6–11 stresses Christ's willingness despite being in the form of God and equal to God to empty himself and be born in human form, eventually being exalted and worshipped by all whether in heaven, on earth, or below the earth. Colossians, perhaps, is farther down the road, but has not traveled out of Pauline territory. Moreover, the emphasis on cosmic Christology may be part of a rhetorical strategy urging the audience to trust that Christ had accomplished all that was needed for salvation, that participation in this exalted Christ exalted the members of his body. Nonetheless, for some, the emphasis on Christ's triumph over rulers and authorities (Col 2:15) blunts an emphasis on Christ's parousia or coming again as the moment of complete victory in the undisputed letters (e.g., Lohse [1968] 1971, 179). Moreover, Colossians' description of Christ as the head of the body of the church may stray from the way Paul speaks of the church as the body of Christ in 1 Corinthians and Romans (see e.g., Brown 1997, 612; Furnish 1992, 1094; Lohse [1968] 1971, 179). These latter two points relating Christology to eschatology and ecclesiology lead to further discussion of those categories.

Eschatology

Considering eschatology first, many scholars argue that "genuine" Pauline eschatology maintains a tension between the "already" and the "not yet." A new age has dawned with the death and resurrection of Christ. Christians already live in this new age of grace and life. Yet, the new age is not yet fully here. Christians await its full arrival with Christ's second coming, which in some letters appears to be imminent. In 1 Corinthians, for example, we read that "the present form of this world is passing away" (1 Cor 7:31b, NRSV) and Christ's resurrection is the first fruits and at his coming those who belong to him will be raised (1 Cor 15:20–26). First Thessalonians 4:13–18 announces that when the resurrected Lord returns, the dead in Christ will rise and the living will join them, meeting the Lord in the air. Romans 6:3–5 suggests that having died with Christ in baptism (already), Christians will rise with Christ in the future (not yet). Colossians, some argue, emphasizes a realized eschatology rather than an already/not yet one and so cannot come from Paul himself (see discussion in Barclay [1997] 2004, 26; Brown (1997), 612–613; Dunn 1996, 36; O'Brien 1982, xlvi–xlvii; Standhartinger 2010, Sect. 3.1; Sumney 2008, 5–6). In Colossians, Christians already live in the empire of God's son. Having been buried with Christ in baptism, the Colossians have already risen with Christ as well (Col 2:9–15; 3:1).

This emphasis on new life in the present, however, can be explained as a stress on the sufficiency of Christ as a response to assertions that the Colossians need to observe particular festivals, engage in ascetic practices, and experience visions. Yet, even in that context, the observances and practices are dismissed as shadows of what is coming (2:17), suggesting a future reality. There are also other elements of future eschatology. Colossians 3:4–6 suggests a future glory and a coming judgment. This may be echoed in 3:24–25, which points to future reward and punishment for masters and slaves. Yet, the pressing imminence of the Parousia (second coming) we find in 1 Thessalonians and 1 Corinthians is not front and center. As Sumney points out, however, there seems to be a trajectory toward less imminence even in the undisputed letters (2008, 6).

In addition to already-not-yet versus future eschatology, there also appears to be a shift from largely temporal imagery in the undisputed letters to the spatial imagery of heaven and earth as in Col 1:20 and 3:2 (Barclay [1997] 2004, 26; Pervo 2010, 67). However, the spatial categories of earth and heaven are also present in the undisputed letters, for example, in 1 Cor 15:40, 47, and 2 Cor 5:1. The Paul of 2 Cor 12:2–6 can even speak of personally being "caught up to the third heaven."

Ecclesiology

One of the obvious differences that might exist between a later letter and the undisputed Paulines, if one assumes increasing institutionalization over time, is mention of a highly developed church order complete with specific offices. This is not present in Colossians (Sumney 2008, 4). If we look to leaders mentioned in Colossians, Nympha has an assembly in her house, Epaphras is a slave of Christ, and Archippus has a ministry to complete. However, for some, as we mentioned in the discussion of Christology, there is a key difference in how Colossians and 1 Cor 12:12–27 and Rom 12:4–5 treat an important metaphor for the church/assembly, the body of Christ. This powerful metaphor stresses that each member of the assembly is a member of the body of Christ. In Colossians, however, Christ is the head of the body (1:18; 2:19) and head over all rulers and authorities (2:10). Further, some interpreters argue that the body of Christ in 1 Corinthians and Romans refers to a local church assembly, whereas the church in Colossians is not only a local body, but also a universal church over which Christ rules as Lord and head (Lohse [1968] 1971, 179; Pervo 2010, 67; cf. O'Brien 1982, xlv and Grindheim 2013, 175–78). On one hand, Colossians uses the same metaphor albeit with Christ as the head. On the other, do we have a development beyond what the Paul of the undisputed letters might say? Questions of theology merge with assumptions about the early Christ assemblies moving toward a greater universalism over time.

Parenesis/ethics

Most interpreters identify a key element of the approach to ethics in the undisputed letters as "the indicative implies the imperative." This means that believers are to respond to what God in Christ has done for them by living a transformed life. This idea is present in Col 3, which describes stripping off the old self and putting on the new self as one strips off old clothing and puts on new clothing (Barclay [1997] 2004, 27–28). The new clothing consists of key virtues, especially love. It also means according to Col 3:11 (NRSV), "there is no longer Greek and Jew, circumcised and uncircumcised, barbarian, Scythian, slave and free; but Christ is all and in all!" However, this destruction of distinctions is followed by a household code, which deals with relations between husbands and wives, masters and slaves, and parents and children in a way that many argue comes from a later stage of church development (e.g., MacDonald 2000, 7–8). Would the Paul of 1 Corinthians who advocated celibacy as long as one could exercise self-control, who promoted unhindered focus on the Lord, and held that each spouse must give the other conjugal rights in 1 Cor 7 enjoin household relations of interlocking dominance and subordination promoted across the Roman Empire as part of common morality? Would the Paul of 1 Cor 7:21 who indicates that slaves should avail themselves of the opportunity of freedom should this become possible counsel submission? When the Paul of 1 Corinthians is presented in this way, the household code of Colossians seems out of character.

On the other hand, 1 Corinthians speaks of the man/husband as the head of the wife/woman (11:3). It also counsels slaves to remain in the condition in which they were called. Similarly, 1 Cor 14:34–35 tells women to learn from their husbands at home. Some think 1 Cor 14: 34–35 is a later interpolation (addition) inserted into 1 Corinthians and not part of the original letter. However, that judgment depends on a decision about what Paul could write and still be Paul (see e.g., Schüssler Fiorenza 1999, 187; 2007, 91–101). If Colossians is included in the undisputed letters, then the imagery of 1 Cor 11 and 14:34–35 may be in tune with the household code. Moreover, some argue that the undisputed letters advocate *spiritual* liberation in Christ as in Gal 3:28 where distinctions between Jew and Greek, slave and free, male and female disappear. This would not mean necessarily that Paul advocated *social* liberation; that is, overturning the social structures of a world that was passing away. This may also be why Col 3:11 (NRSV), which announces that "there is no longer Greek and Jew, circumcised and uncircumcised, barbarian, Scythian, slave and free," can be followed so quickly in 3:18–4:1 by the household code (see e.g., C. J. Martin 1991, 218; Moo 2008, 292–93). As we shall see in a later chapter, there is disagreement about whether the household code of Colossians actually supports, subverts, or both supports and subverts traditional household relations advocated in the Roman Empire. Is the discussion of the ethics of household relations itself anachronistic? Is this something that would only occur as the church accommodated itself to a delayed Parousia and an ongoing life in the empire post-Paul? Interpreters disagree.

Historical context

With the discussion of whether the household code could only emerge after Paul's death, we move to a more direct focus on contextual factors that might date Colossians before or after Paul's death. Many of the theological elements already discussed not only entail similarities and differences from the undisputed letters, but also raise the question of whether the differences are likely to have surfaced after Paul's death, typically dated 62–65 C.E. (Roetzel 1999, 178–83). The parameters there are vague, however. If 65 C.E. is the appropriate cutoff date and Colossians unambiguously mentioned an event that occurred after 65 or referenced a person, group, or term that only existed after 65, the letter (or at least the portion of the letter mentioning it) could not have come from Paul. The nineteenth-century challenges mentioned earlier by Mayerhoff and Baur go down this road. Mayerhoff's interpretation is that Colossians argues against the second-century teachings of a group similar to the Cerinthians (a Jewish Christian, possibly gnostic, group). Baur places the letter in the second century because he thought it conversant with second-century gnostic ideas and that it addressed second-century Ebionite opponents (a type of Jewish Christians). If either were correct about second-century opponents, the historical Paul could not have authored the letter. Today, however, few scholars, as we will see in Chapter 2, find Colossians expressing the ideas of or arguing against any sort of second-century group.

The one event that might lend some specificity as to date is an earthquake or a series of earthquakes that may have struck the Lycus (alternate spellings: Lykos, Lycos) River Valley in Roman Asia Minor, today's Turkey. This river valley included Colossae and its close neighbors, Laodicea and Hierapolis. The source for an earthquake dated ca. 60 C.E. is the Roman historian Cornelius Tacitus in his *Annals* 14.27: "One of the famous cities of Asia, Laodicea, was that same year overthrown by an earthquake, and, without any relief from us, recovered itself by its own resources." Assuming Tacitus's information is correct, notice that this quotation does not mention Colossae or Hierapolis. Support for the idea that Colossae was affected by this earthquake or one shortly after comes from the highly edited and somewhat unstable text of early church historian Eusebius's *Chronicle* dating from the fourth century (Cadwallader 2011, 165). The *Chronicle* indicates that an earthquake destroyed Colossae and Hierapolis along with Laodicea during the reign of Roman emperor Nero, ca. 63–64 C.E. Literally translated, it reads: "In Asia, three cities earthquake destroyed Laodicea, Hierapolis, Colossae" (210; Helm Latin text of 1913, 183). This is supported by Orosius's *Seven Books of History against the Pagans* about a century after Eusebius, but possibly dependent on Eusebius. Orosius reads, "In Asia, three cities, that is, Laodicea, Hierapolis, and Colossae, were destroyed by an earthquake" (7.7; Defferari trans. 1964, 299). These scant passages are why scholars often assume there was an earthquake or several earthquakes striking Colossae ca. 60–64 C.E. The general area is earthquake prone (Kumsari, Aydan, Şimşek, and D'Andria 2015), and it is certainly possible that all three cities suffered damage.

For scholars who want to argue that the Paul of the undisputed letters wrote Colossians, the fact that the letter does not mention or reflect an earthquake ca. 60–64 C.E. may provide evidence that Paul wrote the letter before the earthquake (Reicke 1973, 432). However, for advocates of author fiction/pseudepigraphy the very same earthquake provides evidence for a post-60–64 C.E. date. If we assume that one or more earthquakes may have destroyed or at least contributed to a diminished Colossae in the second half of the first century and beyond, the author may have deliberately addressed the letter to Colossae as there would be no one capable of questioning the letter as an address of "Paul" to the fictive situation (Heininger 2012, 314; Sumney 2008, 10). And/or the letter-writer may have chosen not to refer to the earthquake in order to give the impression that the letter was written during the life of the historical Paul, adding verisimilitude (Lincoln 2000, 580; Wilson 2005, 18, 34). Unfortunately, there is a pox on both houses as there is no certainty that an earthquake *decimated* Colossae ca. 60–64 C.E. nor that Colossae faded into obscurity in the late first century for other reasons. Alan Cadwallader in his recent publications may or may not be correct in all aspects of his interpretation of scholarship, coins, and recently discovered or reinterpreted inscriptions from Colossae. Nevertheless, he makes a very convincing case that a scholarly "axiom" that Colossae more or less gave up the ghost—destroyed by an earthquake and/or gravely diminished in importance in comparison to its close neighbors, Laodicea and Hierapolis—ca. 60 C.E. is wrong (2011). Among the convincing evidence he offers is a late first-century to early second-century inscription on a pedestal dedicated to "Markos, son of Markos, chief interpreter and translator for the Colossians" suggesting Colossae was a flourishing commercial center in need of such services (2011, 170–71). He also points to a late first-century to early second-century *bomos* (monument) honoring one Korymbos for repairing the baths and water channel at Colossae. On it, we can still read thirty lines listing donors (Cadwallader 2011, 172–74; 2012, 110–113). Cadwallader's position appears to be winning the day and receives support from Standhartinger's 2011 entry on "Kolossae" in the online German *Bibellexicon*. There she notes the continuous coinage of Colossae until the middle of the third century. She does, however, still think Colossae was a small town during the Roman period and of less importance than Laodicea and Hierapolis.

Authorship criteria overall

Whether we consider structure, style, vocabulary, theology, or context, students and scholars are confronted with a tennis match with no clear winner. Some of the very same data is used both as evidence that the historical Paul was and was not the author of Colossians. In the absence of a smoking gun such as a reference to persons, practices, or events that clearly postdate the death of Paul, we have only similarities and differences between Colossians and the seven undisputed letters most scholars assign to Paul. The same is true if one compares undisputed letters with one another. There are many similarities and differences between 1 Thessalonians and Galatians, for example. This perhaps is inevitable. The letters are brief documents presented as providing the message of Paul to a particular community or individual when he cannot speak to them in person. Readers construct the historical Paul's biography, rhetoric, and theology by reading a set of letters in the light of one another, the readers' reconstructions of Paul's context, the readers' own concerns and assumptions drawn from their own contexts, and the history of the reception of the letters in particular communities.

Moreover, the discussion relies on the assumption that the seven undisputed letters are in fact authored essentially by a single person, whose vocabulary, style, and theology had enough consistency and coherence over time for similarities and differences to settle the authorship question. As White's *Remembering Paul* (2014) suggests, the construct of the seven-letter "Paul" is ripe for rethinking (cf. Fewster 2014; Pervo 2015). Just so, the assumption of a very high degree of coherence and consistency in the letters given their occasional nature as letters and possible coauthorship or use of secretaries. Beyond issues of method, the lack of consensus raises questions about why the authorship debate has been so passionately pursued for hundreds of years and what difference it might make whether "Paul" wrote Colossians. In what follows, I suggest some reasons why interpreters might care about the authorship of Colossians. I also point to recent work that seeks to move the discussion beyond a singular Paul, not only for Colossians, but also for Pauline traditions more generally.

Why and for what purposes does it make a difference whether Paul wrote Colossians: Reconstructing the historical Paul, his reception, and early church history

Why and for what purposes does it make a difference whether Paul wrote Colossians? For those seeking to write a life of the historical figure Paul or to reconstruct his rhetoric or theology, whether Paul himself participated directly in the composition of Colossians makes a difference. Scholars treat letters they identify as Paul's as primary sources and the canonical Acts as a secondary source in writing his biography. This task requires that any letters that later followers composed be eliminated as primary sources. Once a set is determined, scholars try to put the letters in chronological order to reconstruct the course of Paul's life and travels, often aided of necessity with some reference to Acts. Acts, while not a primary source, contains episodes featuring Paul as well as an arc of his mission. Scholars also try to determine whether Paul's thought and practices changed over the course of his life. Indeed, these possible changes as we have seen are central to the debate over authorship. If Paul wrote Colossians ca. 60 C.E., for example, it may be that he did not expect the end of the current age to be as imminent at the end of his life as he did when he wrote 1 Thessalonians, which is thought to be his earliest letter. This may have shifted his practical advice on celibacy and marriage.

Scholars also reconstruct the relationships that Paul had with the communities he addressed in the letters. This contributes to writing a history of early Christianity as well as to writing a biography of Paul. The letters Paul did not author become evidence for the reception and interpretation of Paul's letters as well as primary sources for reconstructing a part of early Christian history post-Paul. If Colossians was the first deuteropauline (second-generation) letter as many contend, it would offer a key turning point in the reception and reworking of earlier Pauline tradition.

Describing the historical Paul's rhetoric and literary techniques also depends on determining which letters are his. Overall, how does Paul use thanksgivings at the beginning of letters, establish his authority, seek to shape the identity and behavior of community members, use metaphors, or incorporate traditional materials? In Colossians, for example, there is an extended thanksgiving, a possible liturgical or poetic element in 1:15–20, and arguably a different use of the metaphor of the body than in the earlier letters. If we want to establish a unique Pauline style and rhetoric or use our understanding of it in the interpretation of a particular letter, we need to base it on letters that Paul authored. Changes in rhetoric and style whether due to different circumstances that Paul addresses or to different circumstances that a later writer addresses may be of note.

Similarly, in reconstructing Paul's theology, scholars often describe Paul's theology in systematic categories such as Christology, ecclesiology, soteriology (teaching on salvation), eschatology, ethics, and so on based on the views set forth in the undisputed letters. Many also try to discover a center or reigning focus to the theology they reconstruct. Deuteropauline letters become evidence for later developments in theology. Colossians, as we have noted, for example, discusses the preexistence of Christ as well as his role in creation and the sustaining of the universe. If Paul authored Colossians, it provides significant input on his cosmic Christology. It might decenter justification by faith or apocalyptic as the beating heart of Pauline theology. If one of Paul's colleagues or a later follower wrote Colossians, on the other hand, scholars can use the letter to reconstruct the ways in which later theologians extended and modified the theology of the undisputed letters.

Religious and ideological influences

In addition to interpreters' interests in reconstructing the life of Paul, his rhetoric and style, or his theology, readers have religious and/or ideological investments in whether Paul composed letters attributed to him alone or with colleagues. Indeed, for many scholars these interests intertwine. For some Christians who believe the books of the Bible are both divinely inspired and without error, if Col 1:1 indicates that Paul and Timothy were the senders of the letter, then they were. To challenge this is to question the divine nature and reliability of Scripture. In addition, as Seesengood explains, Christians who "have a historically rooted faith" often lean toward Pauline authorship and hold the burden of proof to be on those arguing non-Pauline authorship (2010, 47). Other Christians, while still committed to divine inspiration, have no trouble with the idea of Colossians coming from a follower of Paul, particularly if the author was trying to honor Paul, preserve his gospel, or apply it to a new situation. For many, the guarantee of inspiration and authority is whether the church canonized a letter. Although one may and should still distinguish between letters authored by Paul and by followers, the canonical collection of all the letters is significant and a context in which the church should read each of them (Childs 2008, esp. 92–94). To be frank, whether believers find the claim that Paul did not write Colossians troubling sometimes depends on their interpretive community. If one's trusted teachers or denominational curriculum teaches that lying behind Isaiah are at least two prophets from different time periods and that there are several deuteropauline letters, the idea that Paul did not write Colossians is not distressing. On the other hand, if one is taught that to question Pauline authorship is to question the reliability of Scripture, then the suggestion is very much a problem.

Similarly, if either interpreters or their interpretive communities find some letters more central for theology or ideology than others, authorship becomes crucial. Baur's distinction between the principle letters of Romans, Galatians, and 1 and 2 Corinthians and the disputed letters essentially marked a canon within the canon. These along with other letters today considered undisputed are often treated as more theologically significant and sometimes more theologically normative than disputed letters like Colossians or 1 Timothy. For some, the historical Paul has more authority than his followers or those who want to claim Paul's authority for their own ends. They see a downhill trajectory, a fall from Paul. For some who find justification by faith to be the heart of Paul's theology, for example, Romans and Galatians are touchstones and Colossians is found lacking. This view is reinforced by Protestant thinkers such as Ernst Käsemann who sees "the real Paul" of the seven undisputed letters as an individualist and revolutionary Paul celebrating the priesthood of all believers. This Paul, Käsemann holds, was transformed perhaps necessarily into the Paul of a cultically and institutionally oriented early catholicism (1969, esp. 249–52).

Paul as a singular authority

As we have seen, what those who argue the historical Paul did or did not author Colossians often share in common is a focus on Paul as they reconstruct him from a set of letters. The authority of Paul as author and the authority of interpreters who get Paul "right" are at stake for both scholarly and theological purposes. This is a key reason that the debate over the authorship of Colossians and other Pauline letters remains heated. In part, this stems from a focus on Paul as an individual and a point of origin. The original must outshine any number of what must be but pale imitations. Whether for good or ill, Paul is viewed as almost as important or as important as Jesus for the origin and development of Christianity. Whether Paul is cast as someone who ruined the simple religion of Jesus with dogmatic theology or who brilliantly set forth the meaning of the cross and ensured the survival of the community with a gospel embracing Gentiles and Jews, his importance as an individual and as an author is highlighted (see Roetzel 2015, 167–94, for views on Paul). This focus on a singular, authoritative, and "heroic Paul," as Johnson-DeBaufre and Nasrallah (2011) have labeled it, has been highlighted and challenged by feminist scholars, womanist scholars, and others, as we will see. Before we explore these challenges and the impact they may have on debates over the authorship of Colossians, however, it is worth dwelling on some reasons the singular Paul captures our imagination.

For modern readers, the eighteenth- and nineteenth-century Romantic idea of an author as a unique "genius" expressed by figures such as Wordsworth and Schleiermacher also hangs its mantle over Paul's shoulders, fueling the drive to distinguish "authentic" letters (see Ede and Lundsford 1992, 85; Forster 2015; Kittredge 2003, 328; Stillinger 1991, 3–24). Modern notions of copyright may reinforce this (Ede and Lundsford 1992, 83–85). Modern readers may want to plumb the depths of the mind of Paul rather than that of a follower. But even ancient readers sometimes formed a close relationship with an individual "Paul." The early church father Chrysostom (ca. 347–407 c.e.), for example, as Mitchell (2002) stresses, found Paul spoke powerfully to and through him, although Chrysostom's Paul emerged from all of the Pauline letters. The rhetoric and genre of the letters encourages such identification.

The rhetoric of the letters is designed to mediate the presence of Paul and establish him as a central and singular authority. This rhetoric includes calls to imitate Paul (Castelli 1991) and value his suffering. The very genre of the letters as letters forges a relationship with the implied sender for readers who read over the shoulders of the inscribed recipients. Modern readers influenced by historical criticism often want that relationship to be with a "real" or "historical" Paul rather than a follower. The focus on Paul as a singular authority may explain in part why some find the idea of complex multiple authorship embodied in the secretary hypothesis or even the possibility of the historical Paul delegating the writing of Colossians problematic. Similarly, it may lead scholars to ignore the role of those who collected, copied, edited, and transmitted the letters as shaping the Paul we encounter (Brakke 2016, 386–87; Concannon 2016; Krause 2004, 8).

As scholars such as White (2014) and Seesengood (2010, 223) have suggested, there are certain similarities between the quest for the authentic Paul and the quest for the historical Jesus. Today it is easy for us to argue that Baur looked down the proverbial well to find Paul and saw his own face (Lang 2015). It is much harder to discern our own reflections and the ideological and cultural influences that shape our interpretive communities. Those who spend years reading and studying the letters may begin to hear an authorial voice in much the same way as those who focus on reconstructing the historical Jesus may begin to sense that they can distinguish the *ipsissima verba*, the very words, of the historical Jesus from the set of sayings they attribute to him. Thus, they may or may not hear the voice of Paul in Colossians as they have heard it in the set of letters that have taught them to recognize it (Lang 2015). This is likely a matter of both mature scholarly judgment and personal investment. Of course, the *voice* is something we as interpreters construct as we interact with the text. We become storytellers who tell stories of Paul or of a fictional author and his (almost always his) interactions with the original and subsequent audiences. As tellers of these stories, we feel a bond with the author, whose stories we tell. This makes our stories come alive as Margaret Mitchell (2002) has pointed out in her work on the fourth-century interpreter and lover of Paul, Chrysostom, mentioned above. For Chrysostom, a loving bond between himself and the Paul who speaks to him in the letters "ensures the reliability of his interpretation" (Mitchell 2002, 38). In a homily (sermon) on Colossians, for example, Chrysostom conjures up a portrait of Paul in chains based on Col 4:18's "Remember my chains" (NRSV) and ties this to Paul's tears described in Acts 20:31 (Mitchell 2002, 186). This vivid portrait then becomes the basis for public exhortation to consider one's sins, especially sins against those lower than oneself (Mitchell 2002, 186–87). Thus, Paul speaks to and through Chrysostom, who holds up the portrait of Paul to his own auditors, claiming Paul's authority. This experience was likely not unique. Brakke notes that some pseudepigraphers may have identified so closely with their predecessors that writing in their names was for them a spiritual practice (2016, 379, 383–90). He suggests that Paul's call for followers to imitate him (1 Cor 11:1) may have inspired the choice to write as Paul (2016, 386).

Moreover, it may not only be ancient interpreters who think they portray the thought of the historical Paul authoritatively. Mitchell, for example, proposes that modern interpreters engage in a process of painting a portrait of Paul similar to that of Chrysostom, often in opposition to the portraits others have painted (2002, 423–36). These modern interpreters sometimes like Chrysostom tell stories of Paul speaking through all the letters attributed to him including Colossians. As we have noted, others hear Paul only through a set of letters they deem to represent his authentic voice. Each also paints with the colors of the methods they use and a backdrop of reconstructed ancient and modern contexts. The drive to argue that the Paul of Colossians is or is not the "real" Paul may say as much about us as it does about attribution. Moreover, identification with Paul can lead us to claim Paul's authority for our own interpretations as Schüssler Fiorenza points out (1999, 185). This does not mean that the stories of Colossians that interpreters tell are simply fantasies. Rather they suggest that we should practice humility, recognizing that the portraits we paint and the stories we tell involve disciplined imagination (Mitchell 2002, 428–33). We should welcome conversation and criticisms of our reconstructions from a wide variety of perspectives. Further, we might begin to widen our focus to include more emphasis on the diverse communities Paul and his interpreters interacted with from the first century on. The stories of Colossians begin but do not end in the first century.

Beyond a singular Paul and homes for Colossian stories

While there is a long history of focus on Paul as a singular author, recently many scholars have pointed out that this tends to blur our view of the diversity and complexity of the early assemblies. They have reconstructed multiple voices represented within Pauline and deuteropauline letters as well as the voices of the interpreters of Paul within the New Testament and beyond. Feminist, womanist, and cultural critical interpreters have played a key role in this. So have those who study reception history, the interpretation of letters and stories about Paul in various settings over time. While sometimes still relying on determining the authorship of Colossians, placing Colossians in this larger context highlights its contributions to an energetic and varied early Christian conversation as well as to a rich history of interpretation.

Let us turn first to feminist scholars who decenter or recenter Paul to locate him among the many spirited and sometimes contentious members of the early Christ assemblies. These scholars point out that while Paul remains important, even the undisputed letters are coauthored in the sense that they embody conversations between Paul and other early Christ followers. Just a quick glance at the opening, thanksgiving, and closing sections of the letters indicate that Paul had many coworkers and conversation partners including women. Feminist scholars such as Schüssler Fiorenza (1999, 2007), Kittredge (2003), Kittredge and Columbo (2017), Bugg (2006), Concannon (2016), Johnson-DeBaufre and Nasrallah (2011), and Krause (2004) seek to make them come alive by employing several interpretive practices.

One practice is to focus on the voices embedded in the earlier traditions Paul or his followers incorporate in the letters. Examples are christological hymns/poems such as Phil 2:6–11 and what might be a baptismal formula in Gal 3:28 (Kittredge 2003, 323; Krause 2004, 23–24). In Colossians, the poem or hymn in 1:15–20 may reflect a pre-Pauline liturgical tradition with language and ideas the letter-writer responds to and modifies (Kittredge and Columbo 2017, 149–52). Another voice of tradition may appear in Col 3:11, which resembles Gal 3:28 and 1 Cor 12:13. The incorporation of earlier traditions is what Love, who writes on authorship attribution, might label a form of collaborative or "precursory" authorship (2002, 40–41).

Another feminist practice is to reconstruct the voices of members of the communities who work alongside Paul or who represent alternative points of view. The Corinthian women prophets Wire reconstructs from 1 Corinthians and the speaking women that Krause recovers "between the lines" of I Timothy's attempts to silence them are obvious examples of the latter (Kittredge 2003, 326; Krause 2004, 13; Wire 1990). Colossians pictures persons such as Epaphras and Nympha as part of a Pauline network of support. The voices of those who sought visions, practiced asceticism, and celebrated certain festivals and Sabbaths described in Col 2:8–23 may represent a group or groups in Colossae whose ideas the letter opposes or are a construct representing people or ideas extant elsewhere. If Colossians is a product of a Pauline school of followers of the historical Paul, then the letter itself represents part of a larger ongoing conversation (Johnson-DeBaufre and Nasrallah 2011, 171).

Lying behind these feminist interpretative practices is a model of the early Christ assemblies and texts as sites of polyvocal conversation. This model takes the diversity of early Christ believers seriously as a historical context. It also values the polyphony of voices interpreting the letters over time including those of modern interpreters. These feminist scholars are committed to understanding both early Christ believers and later interpreters as engaged in a conversation inclusive of differing perspectives including those of marginalized people. For most, the interpretation of letters like Colossians in contemporary faith communities is as important as historical reconstruction, which is always tentative. There is also a recognition that readers bring differing experiences and assumptions to the process of interpretation. As modern communities are multiple, so were Pauline communities; as Pauline communities were multiple, so are ours. Their view is that historical reconstructions and scriptural interpretations are likely to be richer for entertaining a wide range of views.

The polyphony these feminist interpreters find in the Pauline tradition is also a key note sounded by recent interpreters focused on reception history, which studies how letters and stories about Paul are interpreted over time. There are many Pauls circulating already in the first and second centuries. Daniel Marguerat in "Paul after Paul: A (Hi)story of Reception," writes about the reception of Paul between 60 and 100 C.E. He identifies three poles of a multiform tradition: documentary, biographical, and doctoral (2013, 6). The documentary pole views Paul as a letter-writer. It involves the copying, editing, and collection of Paul's letters. The biographical pole celebrates Paul's life and primarily takes the form of oral tradition reflecting the social memory of the early communities and Paul's practices. Some of this tradition eventually issues in the canonical Acts and the noncanonical Acts of Paul. The third pole is the doctoral pole. It sees Paul as a "doctor of the church," "a theological icon" (2013, 6.) This pole stems from the reading and rereading of the undisputed letters and is reflected in the deuteropauline and the pastoral letters (2013, 6). The pictures of Paul circulating around these three poles both shift and cohere with one another to varying degrees (2013, 21).

Another interpreter focused on reception, Pervo, writes about *The Making of Paul: Constructions of the Apostle in Early Christianity* from the collection and editing of early letters as well as traditions about Paul through Irenaeus. He sees Paul as "a master of polyphony" in integrating diverse voices in early Christianities as well as someone who provoked a variety of responses (2010, 235). Seesengood in his very readable *Paul: A Brief History* (2010) traces the reception of Paul through the twentieth century. White in *Remembering Paul* (2014) focuses on the many competing images of Paul in the second century and relates this to the desire to uncover a "real" Paul from the canonical Paul in modern scholarship beginning with Baur. Baur, as we discussed above, popularized the concept of a set of undisputed letters. White applies social memory theory to Pauline traditions in a way similar to the way some historical Jesus scholars are now approaching their tasks. Whether this proves to be the most fruitful approach in the long run remains to be seen. Nonetheless, he certainly raises key questions for interpretation.

Turning from reception history of the Pauline tradition as a whole, there are also studies of how particular letters and stories of Paul come to be interpreted and applied in many subsequent situations. For Colossians, a particularly effective example is womanist Clarice J. Martin's 1991 work on how the New Testament household codes including Col 3:18–4:1 were used to justify American slavery and how the African American churches rejected such justifications, even while in some cases reading the codes as establishing male headship over women. Here we see the ongoing impact of the reception of Pauline tradition, a topic we will return to in Chapter 3.

What the moves beyond a singular Paul in both feminist and reception historical studies do is to place Colossians in a much larger context, both in terms of the early assemblies and beyond. The debate over authorship, which may never be settled definitively, recedes in importance; how various stories of Colossians are told and to what ends become more important. Nonetheless, as we have seen, a surprising and significant contribution of the authorship debate is a great deal of agreement about the letter's vocabulary, style, structure, and theology even when this leads to differing conclusions. In the next chapter, we turn to the rhetoric and structure of the letter to explore a story of what the letter does and how the letter persuades. We also ask about a matter almost as hotly debated as authorship, whether there is a group Colossians opposes and, if so, who were they?

Rhetoric and Opposition

Exercise One—James Baldwin's "A Letter to My Nephew"

James Baldwin's "A Letter to My Nephew" (1962) is a modern American open letter (a letter intended for a public audience, but which may be addressed to an individual or a small group). It is readily accessible online at https://progressive.org/magazine/letter-nephew/ and elsewhere. You can also find it in Baldwin's best-selling book, *The Fire Next Time* ([1962] 1993), where it is titled "MY DUNGEON SHOOK: Letter to My Nephew on the One Hundredth

Anniversary of the Emancipation." Analyzing this modern letter may help you to recognize the rhetoric of the first-century letter to the Colossians.

While reading Baldwin's letter underline sentences that reveal the problems, questions, issues, and the people it addresses. Also, underline repeated words and phrases. How do these repetitions function as part of the letter's power? How might they shape the sound of the letter if read aloud? Look also for answers to the following questions: What passages paint pictures in words? What comparisons and contrasts stand out? What examples or short narratives does the letter include? How does it portray Baldwin? How does this portrait affect your response? What other individuals or groups are characterized? What functions do these characterizations play? What allusions to literature, music, and historical events can you find? (Note: the line, "The very time I thought I was lost, my dungeon shook and my chains fell off," comes from the spiritual, "You Got a Right." [Johnson and Johnson 2002, 183–84], which itself may allude to Acts 16:26, where an earthquake opens prisoners' chains.) After having done this detailed analysis, create an outline of the letter. What criteria did you use to create the outline? Based on the letter alone, how would you reconstruct the circumstances it responds to or creates? What audiences do you think the letter aims at or creates? How might different people you know react differently to the letter? Why do you think Baldwin casts this open letter as a letter to his nephew?

What effect does knowing that Baldwin (1924–1987) was a distinguished African American queer novelist, essayist, and playwright have on your analysis? That he first published the letter in *The Progressive*, an American magazine promoting social justice and nonviolence, on January 1, 1962? The letter often appears in textbook anthologies and is assigned in classes. What effect might reading the letter in those contexts have? How might a study of the culture of the United States in the 1960s shape your reading of the letter? What role do you think reconstructing the historical context should play in interpreting the letter?

Exercise Two—The letter to the Colossians

Read Colossians in a modern translation or in the latest scholarly edition of the New Testament if you read Greek. Repeat the analytic steps in paragraph two above. This will allow you to start with your own analysis before reading about the interpretations of others.

After you complete your analysis, begin to reflect on what role you think reconstructing the historical context of Colossians should play in interpreting the letter. Consider what roles reading Colossians in the context of the New Testament canon or settings such as a university classroom or church bible study might play. Finally, how do you think your own personal or cultural experience may shape your interpretation?

Introduction

Chapter 1 introduced stories interpreters tell about Colossians. One of these stories told of Paul dictating and sending the letter to the assembly of Christ believers at Colossae. Another told of a fictive author writing a heavenly letter transmitting the presence and teaching of Paul shortly after his death to addressees who may or may not have lived in Colossae. We then focused on the authorship debate and why it has been so central to interpretation. This chapter focuses on the rhetoric and structure of the letter. It tells a story of what the letter does and how the letter persuades. It also explores questions almost as hotly debated as authorship. Does the letter address teachings and practices of a group or an individual it opposes? If so, can we identify them?

There are many rhetorical approaches to New Testament letters that are worth exploring (e.g., see Aletti 2011; Aune 2003, 162–68, 422–25; Given 2010; Klauck 2006, 183–227; Lampe 2010; T. Martin 2015; Penner and Lopez 2012). Here, I borrow some basic concepts from those approaches including concepts used in modern rhetorical analysis. One is the model of a *rhetorical situation*. This concept is implicit in classical rhetoric and is central to modern rhetoric since the late 1960s. It views rhetoric as a communication process involving sender(s), receivers, and message in a specific context. Senders address or create an *exigence*, an issue, question, problem, or event (Aune 2003, 422–25; Porrovechio and Condit 2016, 155–57). The communication process also constructs the identities of sender(s) and receivers through their interaction (Aune 2003, 424; Porrovechio and Condit 2016, 156–57). The context may be historical and cultural, but it may also involve expectations about rhetorical form (Brock, Scott, and Chesebro 1990, 288). Readers familiar with gospel narrative criticism will recognize that this model of the rhetorical situation resembles Seymour Chatman's narrative communication model and variations thereof (1978).

In that model, a real author and real reader communicate via a narrative, which contains additional communicative elements including an implied author, implied reader, narrator and narratee (Malbon 2008, 32; Thatcher 2008, 22). As with the gospels, letter interpreters construct the implied senders and recipients as they ask how the letters impact the original and later audiences.

In asking about the persuasive impact of a message, rhetorical approaches often employ three concepts from Aristotle's *Rhetoric* 1.2.3–6: *ēthos*, *pathos*, and *logos*. Ethos refers to character and persuades by portraying the writer or speaker in a positive light. Pathos appeals to emotion. Logos offers logical proofs or arguments. In addition to persuasive appeals, both ancient and modern analyses look for persuasive *devices* such as repetition, painting pictures with words, comparison and contrast, examples, and stories.

When interpreters focus on persuasion of the first audience, they try to reconstruct the rhetorical situation in an original historical and cultural context. This process involves disciplined imagination. Two images are often used to describe it: a telephone conversation and a mirror. Scholars compare reading a Pauline letter to listening to one side of a telephone conversation (e.g., Francis and Meeks 1973, 1; Hooker 1973, 314). We imagine what the unheard party is saying by listening to the side of the conversation we can hear. This metaphor minus the telephone is very much like one found in a very early guide to letter style, Demetrius's *On Style* (ca. second century B.C.E. to end of first century C.E.). *On Style* explains that a letter is like one side of a dialogue, a written conversation (Klauck 2006, 184–88). It also says that a letter is different from a speech or a philosophical treatise and reveals an image of the writer (*On Style* 227, in Klauck 2006, 185). Thus, a letter's persuasive strategy relies heavily on ethos. The other modern image for a Pauline letter is the text as a mirror in which we see the reflections of the people addressed and of people and arguments opposed (Barclay 1987, 73–74). If the sender is offering advice, we might look for reflections of issues the addressees or the sender have raised (Gupta 2012, 362–64).

Whether we view the text as a conversation or a mirror, if our interest is historical, a major problem is that all we have is one side of the conversation and possibly a distorted mirror. We read over the shoulders of an implied sender and recipients. They become the signposts for actual senders and recipients. Further, we employ our own personal and cultural ears and eyes. Reconstructions of the implied rhetorical situation and through it the original historical situation remain tentative and subject to revision.

Reconstructing the rhetorical situation as a historical situation—Guidelines

As the images of one side of a conversation and the letter as mirror indicate, reconstructing the original addressees and the situation embodied in Colossians is difficult. Lively discussion ensues precisely because we are dealing with probabilities rather than certainties. Disputes about the best methods for reconstruction are frequent. Among the best discussions of method are those of Barclay (1987), Dahl (1967), Gupta (2012), and Sumney (2005b). To them should be added discussions of the social location of interpreters and audiences including interlocking categories such as age, economic status, ethnicity, gender, religion, and sexuality (e.g., Schüssler Fiorenza 1999, 2007; Buell and Johnson Hodge 2004; Oakes 2012). Influenced by these discussions, the following are some key guidelines relevant to Colossians:

1 The letter represents the sender's perspective. The letter may caricature people or positions with which the sender disagrees, particularly in polemical (hostile) contexts. Reconstructions must take this into account.

2 The internal implied rhetorical situation should guide historical reconstruction. We should examine the letter itself before turning to other texts or social or cultural information to color in or outside of those lines.

3 Explicit and direct statements within the letter about addressees, issues, and possible opponents should serve as a starting point. Other statements must be assessed on a case-by-case basis. For example, if the letter discusses baptism, it does not *necessarily* mean that the audience has questions about baptism or that opponents are urging a different interpretation of baptism.

4 The first-century audience and any opponents may not reflect a single viewpoint or social location. Just as in a modern voluntary association such as a church or a club, there were likely assembly members with similar experiences and interests, but who also differed in other ways. In Colossians, we might imagine a recipient who owns a wool-dyeing workshop and another who is a leather worker living at subsistence

level. We might imagine a Phrygian male slave child and a Roman slave-owning widow. We might imagine a Greek former Cynic and a member of a Greek-speaking Jewish association.

5 Just as the ancient audience was not homogenous, so also later audiences are not homogenous. Interpreters should consider how their own social location and commitments shape their reconstruction.

Establishing a rhetorical situation—Colossians 2:6–23 as a key

Given the methodological guidelines outlined above, we will begin reconstructing a rhetorical situation with explicit verses in Col 2:6–23. For many interpreters, this passage tells the story of teaching and practices that present the central problem of the letter—whether these teachings and practices were reported to Paul and Timothy, are the target of a fictive author in a later context, or may even themselves be fictive. Typically, interpreters take the passage to represent actual teaching and practices the letter opposes. Colossians 2:8 warns the recipients: "See that no one takes you captive through philosophy and empty deceit according to human tradition, according to the elements of the cosmos and not according to Christ." Verse 16 admonishes: " do not let anyone condemn you regarding food or drink or festivals, new moons, or Sabbaths." Further, "Do not let anyone willfully disqualify you through the humility and worship of angels, which things he has seen when entering [. . .]. He is puffed up for no reason by his fleshly mind" (2:18 a and b, translation of Sumney 2008, 149). The letter goes on to pose a rhetorical question asking recipients why submit (alt. why have you submitted) to regulations, "'Do not handle, Do not Taste, Do not touch'" (2:20–21, NRSV). It asserts this human teaching only appears to offer wisdom, "with self-imposed worship, humility, and severity to the body" that does not "prevent gratification of the flesh" (2:22–23).

Most recent interpreters take these verses as a description of a philosophy that involves asceticism, possibly dietary rules, and the observance of certain holy days—whether that of an individual or a group, and whether outside or inside the assembly. Many hold that ascetic practices lead to an altered state of consciousness in which ascetics have visions in which they join in the worship of angels. The term "philosophy" may or may not come from the ascetics themselves. It also does not necessarily mean that the ascetics adhere to a Hellenistic philosophical system like Cynicism or Middle Platonism, although it may. (The Jewish historian Josephus famously used the term philosophy to describe Jewish Essenes, Sadducees, and Pharisees as sects or parties [*Ant.* 18:11–23; *War* 2:119–66].) Two of the phrases in the passage have prompted much debate: "worship of angels" and "elements of the cosmos."

Does worship of angels mean that the philosophy involved worshipping angels? Or, venerating angels and calling on them for protection and help (e.g., Arnold [1996] 2015, 90–102)? Or, that ascetic visionaries joined angels in worship in the heavens (e.g., Francis 1973a, 163–96; Sumney 2008, 11, 154–56)? This issue arises because the phrase worship of angels (*thrēskeia tōn angellōn*) could refer to any of these options in the first century. The translation of the Greek phrase is also difficult. The technical question is what type of genitive is intended. A similar issue arises in English. Take the phrase "the worship of Jesus." Does this mean worshipping Jesus or Jesus's worship of God?

Turning to "elements of the cosmos" in 2:8 and 2:20, what might this phrase have meant to first-century addressees? Does it refer to elemental spirits in parallel to the rulers and authorities mentioned in 2:10 and 15, the angels of 2:18, and/or the "thrones or dominions (lordships) or rulers or authorities," mentioned in 1:16 earlier in the letter? Galatians 4:3 and 9 support this view if the phrase there means supernatural beings that enslaved believers before Christ. Interpreters who reject "elemental spirits" argue, however, that there are no texts prior to the second century where the meaning is elemental spirits. Therefore, we should not translate elemental spirits here or in Galatians. Moreover, many texts do describe the elements of the world as earth, water, air, and fire (Schweizer 1988, 455). The phrase in Colossians might align with texts in which earth, water, wind, and fire were in disharmony and could tie souls to the world after death without ascetic practices—something the Colossians might fear (Schweizer 1988, 467). A third alternative is to read elements (*stoicheia*) simply as elementary teaching, principles, or building blocks. This is a common use in the first century (Sumney 2008, 131). Together with cosmos read as "world," the teachings the letter opposes would be elementary and worldly rather than divine (Sumney 2008, 131; Witherington 2007, 155). A fourth alternative combines elemental spirits with the elements earth, water, air, and fire. Hellenistic thought conceived of these elements as "under the control of spirit powers" and as forces of fate (Lincoln 2000, 565). A number of texts prior to the late first century embody this view. Wisdom of Solomon 13:2, for example, explains that the Gentiles believe that these elements are gods that rule the world (Talbert 2007, 211).

No matter how first-century recipients understood worship of angels and elements of the cosmos (and they may not have all agreed), the letter firmly opposes the teachings and practices described in 2:6–23. It warns with a strong metaphor against being taken captive. This metaphor would have been striking to slaves captured in war, perhaps even slaves in the letter's audiences (Kittredge and Colombo 2017, 169). The passage also powerfully and repeatedly contrasts the philosophy as deceitful human tradition with the divine origins of what the Colossians had been taught and their life in Christ. It stresses Christ's victory, which they share through baptism. This victory brings forgiveness and joins them into a body with Christ as its head, an echo of 1:18. The passage contains a narrative of Christ's death and resurrection and what it accomplishes for believers, recalling previous passages in the letter. Vivid metaphors carry the message. In Christ, the Colossians have been circumcised with a circumcision not made with hands. This metaphor for baptism may allude to passages from the Jewish Bible such as Deut 10:16, Jer 4:4, and Ezek 44:7 (MacDonald 2000, 99). In Col 2:11, the baptized have stripped off the body of flesh as if removing a garment, a metaphor echoed in 3:9. They have died, been buried, and raised. In verse 14, God has erased the *cheirographon*, an IOU signed by a debtor (Talbert 2007, 214), "a record of sins" (Sumney 2008, 144) by nailing it to the cross, a vivid pictorial image. Slaves and the free poor bound by a literal *cheirographon* might have particularly resonated with this image (D'Angelo 1994, 320). In verse 15, God has stripped (disarmed) rulers and authorities leading them as captives in a triumphal procession, just as the Romans publically displayed and shamed those they defeated and enslaved (MacDonald 2000, 104; Sumney 2008, 147). These vivid metaphors provide a sharp contrast between the passage's portrayal of what the Colossians had been taught and life in Christ on one hand and the teaching and practices of the ascetics on the other. Given the contrast, some interpreters find identity to be a central issue at the heart of the rhetorical situation in addition to or instead of opposition to teachings or practices (e.g., Canavan 2012; Shkul 2013). One function of the letter's rhetoric, and one of the things the letter does, is to construct an identity it encourages recipients to embrace via contrast.

As we will see, the letter prepares for the contrast between the gospel it argued the Colossians had received and lived in Christ and the teaching and practices of the ascetics in previous sections of the letter. It does this through an introductory greeting and thanksgiving in 1:1–23 that praises their faith and seeks to establish a shared understanding of it. The letter's thanksgiving and a portrait of Paul in 1:24–2:5 also link the addressees to the apostle. These passages appeal to ethos and pathos. They encourage the first and later recipients to trust Paul as one who has suffered and struggled for them even though they have never seen him face to face. The letter also follows the contrast in 2:6–23 with ethical exhortations that stem from it, describing how one should live in Christ.

Given that the letter's overall persuasive strategy constructs an opposing view, several cautions are in order as we noted above. If this view reflects a real individual or a group, it may caricature the view and people who held it. Jews as well as Jewish and Gentile Christ followers have pursued an ascetic path and visions. Indeed, the Corinthian correspondence describes a preference for celibacy and Paul himself being caught up into the third heaven and into paradise (1 Cor 7:7–8; 2 Cor 12:2–4). There may have been a group that promoted an ascetic lifestyle, visions, and observance of certain holy days that Paul or a fictive author opposes. Whether such a group thought these practices were required for forgiveness is an open question. Colossians 2:6–23 portrays a group failing to embrace Christ's death and resurrection and baptism into Christ as sufficient. The letter's rhetoric has persuaded interpreters who speak about Colossian "errorists," a "false teaching," or a Colossian "heresy" when there was not yet a reigning orthodoxy. Other interpreters as we shall see have a less negative view.

Before turning to various historical reconstructions of the audience and possible opponents, it is important to consider the overall structure of the letter and how other passages contribute to its rhetoric as well as provide additional clues. Along the way, we will attend to metaphors and verbal echoes that connect passages and reinforce themes. We will also highlight passages whose interpretations are contested. First, however, a brief discussion of letter form and rhetorical form is needed.

Rhetoric and structure

Many interpreters note that Colossians follows the standard form of Pauline letters to assemblies with a greeting, thanksgiving, body, ethical exhortations, and closing (for an introduction to the form, see Roetzel 2015, chapter 3). Interpreters quibble over where each part begins and ends precisely. For example, some hold the Thanksgiving section runs from 1:3 to 1:23 while others hold that it is shorter. They might label 1:3–8 as the Thanksgiving followed closely by a section of intercession in verses 9–11 (e.g., Lohse [1968] 1971, vii). Nonetheless, a typical outline of Colossians might include the Greeting in 1:1–2, the Thanksgiving in 1:3–23, the Body in 1:24–2:23, Ethical Exhortations in 3:1–4:6, and the Closing in 4:7–18. This outline helps us to understand how the sender(s) engage the audience as recipients of a letter. For example, Pauline thanksgivings typically give thanks for the recipients, foreshadow the concerns of a letter, and often have liturgical elements (Roetzel 2015, 74–76). They establish a positive connection between the sender(s) and the recipients to prime the pump for a positive response and prepare them for what is to come. This is exactly what occurs in Col 1:3–23.

While it is quite common to create an outline of Colossians based on the Pauline letter form, other interpreters analyze Colossians' structure using traditional Greco-Roman parts of speeches sandwiched between a letter opening and closing (e.g., Aletti 2012). After the greeting, for example, Aletti posits an exordium or introduction in 1:3–23 ending with a partitio or outline in 1:21–23. The partitio announces three key themes to be developed including "a) the work of Christ for the holiness of the believers", "b) faithfulness to the gospel received", "c) and announced by Paul" (Aletti 2012, 314). A probatio or section of proofs in 1:24–4:1 follows, treating the themes in reverse order. "Final Exhortations" in 4:2–6 and the letter closing in 4:7–18 follow (Aletti 2012, 314).

While this and similar outlines highlight proofs used to persuade, some question the usefulness of an analysis designed for speeches, not just for Colossians, but also for Pauline letters in general. After all, these are letters even if they were read aloud. Further, the extent to which the letter-writers studied or may have absorbed formal rhetoric in the Greco-Roman air is debated. Nonetheless, interpreters such as Lincoln (2000), Bugg (2006), and Sumney (2008) have combined the letter structure with elements from rhetorical analysis of speeches in their outlines of Colossians. Moreover, we may have a rose by any other name would smell as sweet resolution. For example, whether we label 1:3–23 the thanksgiving or the exordium, the function is the same. Similarly, the section focused on Paul in 1:24–2:5 functions in the same way whether one calls it part of the letter body or a proof. Sumney finesses this well by calling 1:24–2:5 "the first section of the body of this letter's argument" (2008, 95). We will follow his lead, discussing how other passages in addition to 2:6–23 function as parts of a letter and as rhetorical discourse.

Greeting 1:1–2

The greeting establishes the senders of the letter as "Paul, apostle of Christ Jesus through the will of God and Timothy, the brother." The recipients are "holy ones and faithful brothers in Christ in Colossae." Identifying the senders and receivers at the beginning is typical of Greco-Roman letters. This greeting ties both senders and receivers to Christ. The phrase "in Christ" will echo throughout the letter. The greeting also asserts that the source of Paul's authority is God. It also affirms a connection via fictive brotherhood.

Thanksgiving/exordium/introduction 1:3–23

As noted above, most Pauline thanksgivings including the Colossian thanksgiving give thanks for the recipients, broadcast the letter's concerns, and contain liturgical elements. The Colossian thanksgiving establishes a relationship with the recipients and prepares them to respond positively to the rest of the letter. Colossians 1:3–14 gives thanks and offers prayer for the Colossians. The famous "hymn" to Christ in 1:15–20 follows, possibly appealing to a shared liturgical tradition about Christ's creative and reconciling activity. Finally, verses 21–23 include a summary of the three key themes or proofs taken up in the rest of the letter. Repeated words and concepts tie the thanksgiving/exordium together including faith, hope, and gospel in verses 4–6 and 23 (Talbert 2007, 182). The thanksgiving also establishes the connection of Paul and Timothy to Epaphras and through him to the Colossians. This may be a clue to the original historical situation whether the senders are Paul and Timothy or presented as Paul and Timothy by a fictive author. The role of Epaphras as a leader and part of a Pauline network is affirmed here and in the letter's closing in 4:12–13. Some see this as evidence of an added purpose of the letter, that is, to enhance the standing of Epaphras and other leaders, perhaps in the face of Paul's death (MacDonald 2000, 7–8).

In addition to praise for the Colossians' faith, love, and hope, there is a repeated metaphor of bearing fruit. The gospel bears fruit and increases among them as they are to bear fruit in good works. This metaphor might ring bells for addressees familiar with the oral tradition now embedded in Matt 7:16–20/Matt 12:33/Luke 6:43–45 concerning trees bearing fruit. It also might resonate with Roman imperial imagery that ties "fertility and abundance" to the emperor's reign in the world, a different sort of gospel (Maier 2013, 83–85). As the senders describe prayers of intercession for the

Colossians, they begin to outline key concerns addressed later in the letter. They repeatedly ask for growth in the knowledge of God. The senders wish for the recipients to bear fruit, to walk worthily, that is, to live worthy lives, a concern taken up in the ethical exhortations of 3:1–4:6 as well as in 2:6 where they are to walk in Christ. What God has done for them requires no additions. Verse 12 announces that the Father gives them the inheritance of the holy ones in the light. Verses 13 and 14 switch from you to us, announcing that God the Father has "delivered us from the dominion of darkness and transferred us into the empire of his beloved Son, in whom we have redemption, the forgiveness of sins." These claims foreshadow those in 2:6–23, where the forgiveness of trespasses is also assured. For those familiar with the Septuagint (the Greek version of the Jewish Bible), the language of "share" and "inheritance" in verse 12 might evoke the image of God's provision of a share of the promised land as in Deut 10:9, 32:9, and Josh 19:9 (Lohse [1968] 1971, 36; Talbert 2007, 186). The metaphor of an inheritance unexpected for slaves will also appear in 3:24.

With the transition focusing on the Son in 1:13–14, the letter sets the stage for one of the most well-known sections of Colossians, the liturgical poem or hymn of verses 15–20. An exegetical cottage industry has developed around its interpretation. Questions addressed include its structure, whether it is preformed tradition (and if so, whether there are editorial additions), whether it was sung or recited, and what cultural traditions it draws upon. Lincoln (2000, 601–605) has an excellent summary of the literature. Here we are most interested in what this passage does in terms of the rhetoric of the letter, but it is worth dwelling briefly on its structure and origins.

One useful way to see the structure is as two lengthy parallel strophes or stanzas connected by a short middle stanza (Lincoln 2000, 602–603; Talbert 2007: 184). All the stanzas focus on Christ. Below is a somewhat wooden translation leaning on Lincoln and Talbert, and following Talbert most closely. It bolds repeated words and phrases to highlight how repetition knits the passage together:

[FIRST STANZA]
Who is the icon of the invisible God,
Firstborn of all creation
That in him were created **all things in the heavens** and **on the earth**
The visible and the invisible
whether thrones or dominions [lordships] or rulers or authorities
All things through him and for him were created

[INTERMEDIATE STANZA]
And he is before **all things**
And all things in him hold together
And he is the head of the body, the assembly/church (*ekklēsia*)
[FINAL STANZA]
Who is the beginning
Firstborn from the dead
That he might hold preeminence in **all things**
That in him was pleased all the fullness to dwell
And **through him** to reconcile **all things** to himself
Having made peace through the blood of his cross
Through him
Whether things **on the earth** or things **in the heavens**

The passage is a miniature narrative of who Christ is and what he has accomplished, to which the senders can appeal in the rest of the letter. The first and last stanzas place in parallel the role of Christ in creation and redemption. The first stanza celebrates Christ as the icon (image) of the invisible God, his preeminent role in the creation of all things in the heavens and on earth, visible and invisible including thrones, dominions, rulers, and authorities. The latter may represent cosmic powers including heavenly beings and/or earthly rulers, both of which may oppress believers (Keesmaat 2014, 561; Sumney 2008, 67). The final stanza stresses the fullness of God dwelling in Christ as well as Christ's preeminence as the first resurrected, the one who reconciles all things whether on earth or in the heavens, making peace through the cross. The reference to making peace conjures the imagery of Roman imperial peace accomplished through violence as well as parallels between heavenly peace and the peace Rome achieves on earth (Maier 2013, 69–71). Ironically, peace is established via Roman violence in shedding Christ's blood on the cross. For some, it might also call to mind God as the peacemaker, who as Philo, a Hellenistic Jewish thinker, says establishes harmony in cities and in the parts of the universe (*The Special Laws*, II 192, referenced in Talbert 2007, 190). The middle stanza ties Christ's roles in creation and redemption to holding all things together, a sort of cosmic "glue" (Talbert 2007, 189; Witherington 2007, 134). It also connects Christ's roles in creation and redemption to his role as head of his body, the *ekklēsia* (assembly/church), possibly evoking the image of the emperor as head of the civic body (Keesmaat 2014, 561).

Christ's agency in the creation, sustaining, and reconciliation of all things rhythmically proclaimed in the passage very likely has roots in Hellenistic

Jewish wisdom traditions. Christ takes the role that personified Wisdom and the Logos (divine reason) play in these traditions (Lincoln 2000, 605). For example, Wisdom is "the image of God," the firstborn, and plays a role in creation (Lincoln 2000, 605). Further, the Logos "holds all things together," and, according to Philo, is "head of the body, the world of souls, announces God's peace, and mediates between the disparate elements of the universe" (Lincoln 2000, 605).

Whatever cultural repertoire the passage draws upon, the likelihood that it is largely a preformed tradition the recipients know is significant. If it is a tradition they recognize and use in worship, it helps to cement shared values and enhance a relationship with the senders. It serves as a reliable basis for the letter's argument against the teachings and practices 2:6–23 describes as well as for the teaching and practices it advocates. For modern readers, the Christ hymn may provide insights that help to reconstruct the recipients' perspective as part of the rhetorical situation. It may also help to recover other voices alongside the voices of the senders that shaped the life of the early Christian communities. Feminist interpreters might say that the writer has a coauthor, the assembly of saints.

With the end of the poetic/liturgical praise of Christ on the note of reconciliation, the thanksgiving/exordium turns to what Christ has done specifically for the recipients and links it to the hymn/poem. There is a switch back to addressing "you." Christ reconciles the "once alienated and hostile" who did "evil deeds" through his death (1:21–22). Christ renders them blameless *if* they remain established and secure in the faith, trusting in "the hope of the gospel" proclaimed to them and "to every creature under heaven," the gospel to which Paul became a servant (1:22–23). This conclusion echoes what has gone before. It also foreshadows what is to come, outlining the letter's three key themes: (1) what God in Christ has done to make believers holy, (2) that they are to remain in the faith, the gospel they heard, and (3) that Paul is a reliable servant of that gospel (Aletti 2012, 314; Lincoln 2000, 607; Sumney 2002, 344; Witherington 2007, 137). The reference to Paul and the switch to the personal pronoun "I" serves as a transition into the first section of the letter's body, which focuses on Paul and why the audience should trust and side with him.

Body: Ethos, pathos, and Paul—1:24–2:5

The body of the letter begins in 1:24–2:5 with Paul or a pseudepigrapher establishing Paul's credentials. This section paints a picture of Paul's character and creates an emotional connection with the implied audience. It establishes his reliability in contrast to the ascetics of 2:6–23. It appeals to ethos, that is, it sets forth why the recipients should trust this messenger. It also appeals to pathos as it depicts Paul's suffering. There are two subsections: 1: 24–29 and 2:1–5.

Verses 24–29 are one long sentence explaining what Paul does on behalf of his addressees. It explains that God commissioned Paul to bring God's word and make the glorious mystery of God's plan known to the Gentiles, "which is Christ in you, the hope of glory" (1:27, NRSV). Here there might be an indirect clue that the Colossian assembly is made up largely of those of Gentile descent and/or that part of the mystery is that Gentiles are included. At any rate, Paul proclaims this mystery, warning all humans and teaching all humans in all wisdom so that all humans might be perfected in Christ (1:28). His mission ultimately includes all people as the three-fold repetition of all humans emphasizes. Paul works hard, struggling (*agōnizomenos*) as one fighting in a contest, calling to mind the athletic field, the gladiatorial arena, or the courtroom. Paul struggles with all the energy of the one who energizes him in power (1:29). The story told is one of Paul inspired by God mightily working on behalf of the letter's recipients and indeed, on behalf of all to whom he is sent. Thus, Paul's connection to all readers reading over the shoulder of the implied readers is established. Verse 24 also stresses that Paul suffers in his flesh on behalf of Christ's body, the *ekklēsia* (assembly, church).

The way the letter expresses Paul's suffering, however, has caused a great deal of interpretive consternation. In a rather literal translation, 1:24 reads: "Now, I rejoice in sufferings for you and I fill up the lack in Christ's tribulations in my flesh, for his body which is the assembly." This phrase is like fingernails on a chalkboard to many. Could Paul or the fictive author be saying Christ's death was not sufficient and Paul had to add to it? Some take this verse as the fingerprints of a pseudepigrapher, holding that the "real" Paul would not make this claim (e.g., Kiley 1986, 59–60). It would certainly magnify Paul as a heroic apostle and martyr. While this reading might exalt Paul's role, it would detract from the point that the letter stresses throughout that Christ's death accomplished an all-sufficient reconciliation (1:20, 22; 2:12–14, 20).

One common recent reading of 1:24 sees Paul's suffering for others in an apocalyptic key. Paul's suffering helps to complete an appointed amount of suffering before the end comes. Christ's death inaugurated the end times and Paul's suffering identifies him with Christ. It helps to complete the required amount in his mission to share God's apocalyptic mystery with the Gentiles (e.g., Dunn 1996, 114–117). Ringing a change on this, Bauckham and Lincoln argue that the context stresses that Paul's suffering fulfills a lack as part of the mission of the proclamation of the gospel to the whole world that must occur before the end comes (Bauckham 1975, 169–70; Lincoln 2000, 614). Another reading that coheres with the letter's emphasis on being "in Christ" sees Paul sharing in Christ's suffering as he and the faithful in Christ are so closely united. Christ, Paul, and the members of the body are inextricably bound. MacDonald holds that Christ continues to suffer as believers suffer, and Paul suffers on behalf of the community (2000, 79). Horrell, Hunt, and Southgate, reading 1:24 in an ecotheological key, also link Christ, Paul, and the believer: "If the struggles of the apostle have significance for the church in completing the work of Christ, and we recognize from 1:20 the cosmic scope of that work, it seems reasonable to extrapolate to the conclusion that the struggles of the believer, like those of Christ may have liberative force for creation as a whole" (2010, 141). A final interpretation views Paul's suffering in the light of the Greco-Roman concept of the noble death, which leads by example. Sumney argues Paul's sufferings are vicarious, on behalf of others, because they lead others to imitate them, not because they are expiatory (atoning) (2008, 101). They are an example that calls for the recipients to imitate Paul by holding fast to his teaching rather than to that of the ascetics (Sumney 2008, 101). A noble death interpretation would uphold Paul's masculine authority as he is able to endure suffering, to take it like a man. These interpretations of verse 24 are not necessarily mutually exclusive and work whether the historical Paul is alive or dead.

Betz (1995) and Standhartinger (2004, [1999] 2012), however, read verse 24 as a reference to Paul's death. Standhartinger writes that 1:24 is an "attempt to interpret Paul's death theologically" (2004, 580). Paul's death is part of God's plan and he suffers and dies vicariously. Betz writes that "through his martyrdom 'in the flesh' (σάρξ) Paul is 'completing' the continuing afflictions which Christ suffers through his body (σῶμα), identical with the church (1:24)" (1995, 515). According to Betz, however, the believers cannot imitate Paul as they could in the undisputed letters because he is dead. Instead, in Colossians they are united with Christ as they die and rise with Christ in baptism (1995, 516–17).

Returning to our discussion of the overall portrait of Paul, which builds up his character and seeks to draw the recipients' sympathy, the struggling/contesting (agōnizomenos) mentioned in 1:29 serves as a link to 2:1 and the conclusion of the portrait. In 2:1, Paul expresses how great a struggle/contest/

fight (*agōna*) he has been waging on behalf of the Colossians, the Laodiceans, and all those who have not seen his face in the flesh. This effectively includes the Colossians, the neighboring Laodiceans, and all subsequent readers. Paul struggles because he wants their hearts to be encouraged and "knit together in love" so that they will have the wealth and full persuasion of the knowledge of God's mystery in Christ as well as the treasures of wisdom and knowledge found in Christ (2:2–3). Here the notes of the richness of the mystery to be made known in 1:26–27 are sounded again as are the notes of wisdom and knowledge in 1:27–28 and 1:9. Verses 4 and 5 lead into the next section where Paul contrasts the teaching and practices of the ascetics with his own. He is counteracting "plausible," yet deceptive, arguments with his spiritual presence, embodying the topos (standard theme) of a letter substituting for an absent sender. Paul's presence embodied in words functions for the recipients whether its creator is the historical Paul or a fictive author. The story ends on an affirming note rejoicing in the recipients' "good order" (like soldiers lined up in order) and "firmness of faith" (like a strong fortification) in Christ (2:5; see MacDonald 2000, 87 n. 5, for the military metaphors). Expressions of rejoicing, "I am rejoicing in sufferings" and "I am rejoicing" in the recipients, frame and mark off the section (1:24–2:5; Lincoln 2000, 617; Sumney 2008, 119).

At this point, with the strong appeal to ethos as well as pathos concluded, the stage is set for the following section of the letter, which contrasts the teaching and practices of the ascetics with those of Paul. Chapter 2:6–7 states the main point of what is to follow based on what has gone before. It does so in a heap of mixed metaphors. As the recipients have received Christ Jesus as Lord, they are to walk in him, recalling 1:10. The recipients are to be rooted as a plant, built up as on a foundation in Christ, and made strong in the faith they were taught.

Body—Ethical exhortation/parenesis 3:1–4:6

After the section arguing against the teaching and practices of the ascetics and for the teachings and life in Christ the Colossians had received, ethical exhortation (parenesis) follows. The letter develops an alternative lifestyle to that the ascetics advocate. Chapter 3:1–5 uses spatial imagery of above and below to frame the instructions on how to live in the rest of the section. This echoes the vertical imagery of heaven and earth in the Christ hymn.

Since the recipients have died and risen in Christ who sits at the right hand of God above, they should focus on things above. They have already attained what the ascetics seek through their practices. This "already," however, is still connected to a "not yet." Their lives are "hidden with Christ in God," but when Christ is revealed in future glory, so will they be revealed (3:3–4, NRSV). The death and resurrection they have experienced in Christ means they must "put to death" a series of earthly vices, the ways in which they once walked (3:5–8). There are two sets of five vices. The first set concentrates on four sexual sins with a fifth associating greed and idolatry. The vices and the ways once walked might be a clue to an audience of Gentiles since sexual immorality and idolatry are often associated with Gentiles in Pauline letters and Jewish traditions (Drake 2013, 22–23; Dunn 1996, 214). The second set of vices focuses on sins that stem from anger and issue in abusive or foul language. They are not to lie because using the metaphor of putting off and putting on clothing, they are to put off the old self (literally the old human) and put on the new one (3:10). This echoes 2:11 where the Colossians have put off (stripped off) the body of flesh in their dying and rising with Christ in baptism. This imagery continues in verses 12 and 14 that admonish the Colossians to put on (clothe themselves with) five virtues that build up community and above all to put on love (*agapēn*), which will hold them together in perfect unity. As Canavan stresses, putting off old clothing and putting on new clothing is a metaphor for old and new identities (2012, 168–72). The new human is being renewed in knowledge, echoing the importance of knowledge throughout the letter. The new human is also shaped in the icon (image) of the Creator, echoing Christ as the icon (image) of God in 1:15 and likely alluding to Gen 1:26–27. This new life for the community issues in 3:11, "where there is not Greek and Jew, circumcision and uncircumcision, barbarian, Scythian, slave, free, but Christ is all and in all."

Verse 11 closely resembles Gal 3:28 and 1 Cor 12:12–13. This suggests that 3:11 may be a baptismal tradition in which dying and rising in Christ forms a new community. Galatians 3:27–28 even uses the imagery of clothing in relation to baptism. Many interpreters hold that 3:11 abolishes social and ethnic divisions in the community (e.g., MacDonald 2000, 145–48). What is different from Galatians is the addition of "circumcision and uncircumcision, barbarian, Scythian" and the absence of "male and female" (1 Corinthians also lacks "male and female"). Scholars typically read Greek and Jew as opposites paralleling uncircumcision and circumcision in Col 3:11. Both pairs are joined by "and" in the Greek. The rest are simply listed. Should we understand the other listed items as pairs of opposites as well?

Slave and free fits that pattern. However, interpreters have struggled with barbarian and Scythian. To the Greeks all others were barbarians, so the opposition Greek and barbarian would make sense. However, we do not find that opposition. What about the Scythians? The Scythians were nomadic tribes who lived on the Central Asian steppes (Curry 2016; West 2002). Because Scythian was a term used for slaves captured from the northern shores of the Black Sea, Campbell argues Scythian (slave) forms the opposite of barbarian (free) (2014, 272). Sumney, on the other hand, argues that from a Greek perspective Scythian represents a variety of far northern peoples and barbarian represents peoples from the far south (2008, 208–9). Still others hold the last terms are not opposite pairs. Foster sees a list of four representing the destruction of human distinctions (2016, 339–42).

Another possibility is suggested by Buell and Johnson Hodge's reading of Gal 3:28. They argue that Paul establishes a new ethnic-religious identity in Christ, "subordinating a range of social identities to being 'in Christ' " without eliminating them (2004, 248). The new identity incorporates other identities into Paul's Jewish (Judean) ethnic-religious identity (Buell and Johnson Hodge 2004, 247). Their reading would help to explain Colossians' presentation of baptism as "a circumcision made without hands" in 2:11. Greek, Jew, barbarian, Scythian, slave, and free where "Christ is all and in all" (3:11) become "the holy and beloved elect of God" (3:12), language associated in the Jewish Bible with Israel (Dunn 1996, 227–28). These elect clothe themselves with the virtues that accompany that status.

Adding complexity is how this may relate to a Roman imperial cosmopolitanism in which conquest brings peace, unity, and civilization to the diverse peoples under imperial rule. Maier points to the imperial temple at Aphrodisias about 100 kilometers (62 miles) from Colossae as one of several iconographic representations of this view (2013, 77–99). Fifty female statues stand for various nations Rome had conquered (Maier 2013, 87). They are in various stages of being "civilized," as shown through their hair, clothing, and postures (Maier 2013, 87–89). In parallel, Maier writes, "The utopian declaration of Col. 3:11, that includes barbarians and Scythians, is a powerful geopolitical representation of the universal reach of Christ's rule and its power of turning enemies into friends" (2013, 90). Colossians, thus, echoes a Roman pattern its first recipients might recognize. Unlike Roman dominance through violence, however, Christ accomplishes transformation through the cross with Paul as his imprisoned messenger, a powerful counternarrative (Maier 2013, 99–100). Whether this transformation destroys or preserves social and ethnic identities in unity, this message would resonate in the Lycus Valley where Colossae, Laodicea, and Hierapolis were located. There inscriptions offer examples of the hellenizing assimilation of various ethnic groups as part of the Roman civic order as well as the joining of people under the banner of professional trade guilds without abandoning their ethnic identities (Maier 2013, 92–93).

For modern Christian readers, a question to ponder is whether to interpret Col 3:11 as eliminating social, cultic, and ethnic particularities in favor of a universal humanity or as constructing the unity in diversity of a holy, beloved, and elect people. The idea of a universal humanity has often served movements for social justice well. However, a universalizing interpretation has also led to construction of Jews as the opposite and other of a Christian universalism with devastating results (see Buell 2014 and Baker 2017 for some of the complex questions involved).

However one interprets Col 3:11, the absence of "male and female," which is present in Galatians, is also significant. Some find a clue that perhaps the ascetics of 2:6–23 promoted sexual asceticism as a path to females becoming male or to full androgyny (MacDonald 2000, 145–47). Bugg, following Schüssler Fiorenza and others, argues that including the male and female pair as in Galatians would not have promoted androgyny so much as the elimination of patriarchal control of marriage and procreation (2006, 177–83). The letter eliminates the pair male and female that community members might have expected if Col 3:11 is a modification of a traditional baptismal formula. Some in the community understood baptism to eliminate not just spiritual but also social distinctions (Bugg 2006, 178–83).

If the letter uses (and likely modifies) a baptismal tradition in 3:11, what does it use this tradition to accomplish in its context in the letter? The context of 3:1–17 suggests that the purpose is to bind the community together in the light of baptismal transformation. It also contrasts with the letter's portrayal of the ascetics as divisive. Questions about the rhetorical effects remain. Are the distinctions preserved within an overarching unity in Christ or are they destroyed? Is the intent to eliminate distinctions on a spiritual level or also quite literally? For example, are distinctions between slave and free eliminated in daily life? Does the peace of Christ ruling in their hearts in one body (3:15) represent a challenge to the Roman Empire, which depicted itself as bringing peace, civilizing, and uniting diverse peoples in one body with the emperor at its head (Maier 2013, 87–93)? The answers may depend on how one reads the household code, which follows in 3:18–4:1. As we will see in Chapter 3 of this guide, the household code addressing the relationships of wife and husband, child and parent, slave and master may reinforce or challenge hierarchical social relationships, or both.

Following the household code, a few verses form a transition from ethical exhortation to the final greetings and benediction of the letter. Chapter 4:2 urges the recipients to continue in prayer (4:2). Specifically, they are to pray for God to open a door for us—presumably Paul and Timothy—to "declare the mystery of Christ, for which I [Paul] also have been bound" (4:3). Paul is in prison as 4:18 (NRSV) makes clear with the injunction to "Remember my chains." The reason is the declaration of the mystery of Christ, which the letter stresses as Paul's message in 1:26–27 and 2:2. There follows a brief injunction to "walk in wisdom" toward outsiders and to speak graciously "seasoned with salt" in order to know how to respond appropriately (4:5–6).

Closing—4:7–18

The closing of the letter introduces its bearers Tychichus and Onesimus, one of the Colossians, who will bring an oral report. There is then a section of greetings from Aristarchus, "my fellow prisoner;" Mark; and Jesus called Justus. These three are identified as the only fellow workers with Paul, who are among the circumcised (4:10–11). Greetings from Epaphras, already identified in the letter's introduction as the one who taught them the gospel (1:7) follow. Here he is identified as one of them and "a slave of Christ Jesus," who fights for their perfection and assurance in God's will in his prayers (4:12). Paul or the fictive author backs Epaphras as someone who has worked hard for those in Colossae, Laodicea, and Hierapolis (4:13). There are also greetings from Luke, "the beloved physician" and from Demas (4:14). Greetings from Paul to the brothers in Laodicea as well as "to Nympha and the assembly in her house" follow. Final instructions call for reading the letter not only in Colossae, but also in Laodicea, and having a letter sent to Laodicea read in Colossae. The letter concludes with a cryptic call to tell Archippus to fulfill his ministry, a greeting written in Paul's own hand, and a plea to "Remember my chains" (4:17–18, NRSV).

What are the rhetorical functions of this closing? The closing links Paul, who has never met the Colossians, with several persons who they know. This reinforces the reliability of his message. The references to Paul's imprisonment in 4:10–11 and in the plea to remember his chains in 4:18 appeal to ethos and pathos. They reinforce Paul's suffering on their behalf developed earlier in the letter (Sumney 2008, 282). Esler suggests that if the letter was shared after Paul's death in communities subject to persecution, the implied narrative of Paul's imprisonment would serve as a social memory affecting identity in a deeply meaningful way (2007, 254). People often incorporate stories of an important exemplar into the stories of their own lives.

Turning from Paul to the people mentioned, the close association of these figures with Paul might reinforce their authority. MacDonald argues that this closing and the reference to Epaphras in 1:7 reinforce the authority of members of the Pauline network in light of Paul's imprisonment and/or in her view likely death (2000, 35–36, 186–88). The number of persons mentioned also places the recipients among a wide early Christian network of support, which would exist both in Paul's lifetime and after. Similarly, the exchange of letters with Laodicea puts the recipients in a community of assemblies in different locations. Nympha is a significant addition as a woman among the males mentioned, supporting the possibility of leadership or patronage roles for women in the assemblies. The text reads *Nymphan,* which can be male (Nymphas) or female depending on the accent used in the Greek. Some manuscripts read the pronoun her in "her house" as "his" and others as "theirs" (Sumney 2008, 278). Given a scribe is more likely to change "her" to "his" than the reverse, Nympha is the accepted reading much as Junia in Rom 16:7 (Sumney 2008, 278; Wilson 2005, 305).

While the closing may have various rhetorical effects, for many scholars its greatest contribution is to sketch a possible historical context. Seven of the persons—Epaphras, Aristarchus, Mark, Onesimus, Luke, Demas, and Archippus—are also mentioned in Philemon. Not surprisingly, the shared list and the closing autograph in Paul's own hand are read both as evidence that Paul did and did not author Colossians. Those who attribute Colossians to a fictive author argue that the author uses names from Philemon and the autograph to create the impression that Paul authored Colossians. Proponents of Pauline authorship reconstruct a scenario where Paul sends Colossians and Philemon either at the same time or roughly the same time from prison (e.g., Campbell 2014, 263–83; Dunn 1996, 37–41). Both list Paul and Timothy as the senders, but Timothy may have written under Paul's guidance (Dunn 1996, 38–39). Whatever view one takes about authorship, there are, however, differences between the persons mentioned in Colossians and Philemon. Colossians does not mention Philemon and Apphia, and Philemon does not mention Tychicus. Further, Colossians gives greater and sometimes different details about the people. Students who are interested should read Campbell (2014, 276–83) and Balabanski (2015), who deal with these differences in imaginative ways. Campbell argues that Paul writes Philemon and Colossians at the same time from imprisonment in nearby Apamea and intertwines topics related to slavery in both (2014, 263–83). Balabanski argues that the letters were written at different times— Philemon likely in 60 C.E. and Colossians likely by Timothy, two years later, both during an imprisonment in Rome (2015, 145–48). For those who hold some form of authorship by Paul, Rome and Ephesus are the typical candidates for the site of imprisonment.

With the completion of our analysis of the rhetorical situation and this turn to historical context, it is time to explore briefly external clues about audience and possible opponents. A discussion of scholars' reconstructions of the central problem of the letter will follow.

External clues to audience and ascetics

Depending on whether one attributes Colossians to Paul, Timothy, or a fictive author, the destination of the letter may or may not have been Colossae or its neighbors in the Lycus River Valley in Roman Asia Minor (Anatolia) ca. 60–100 C.E. The mention of Colossae, Laodicea, and Hierapolis in the letter, however, suggests the sender(s) were not just throwing darts at a map. They at least know these were neighboring cities on the banks of the Lycus River. Colossae was 18 kilometers (about 11 miles) south of Laodicea (also spelled Laodiceia and Laodikea) and 24 kilometers (about 15 miles) from Hierapolis on the opposite bank of the river (Trebilco 2011, 180). As hellenized cities in the Roman Empire located on major North-South and East-West roads and the Meander river system into which the Lycus flowed, they were well connected and have much in common with many cities in western Asia Minor (Kearsley 2011, 130–31; Şimşek 2017, 2; Thonemann 2013, 8). They form, therefore, a helpful historical backdrop to the letter whether the first addressees were Colossians or not.

Archeologists have never excavated Colossae. Recently, Turkish and Australian scholars have been recovering and publishing inscriptions and other remains from Colossae to reconstruct as much as possible without an actual dig. Especially useful English language works include Cadwallader and Trainor (2011), Cadwallader (2015a, 2015b) and Canavan (2012). Laodicea and Hierapolis have been partially excavated. For Laodicea and

Hierapolis, helpful works in English include Gabellone and Scardozzi (2010), Ritti (2006), Şimşek and D'Andria (2017), and Brandt, Hagelberg, Bjørnstad, and Ahrens (2016). Huttner (2014) reconstructs early Christianity in the Lycus Valley based on archeological and textual data. For anyone fascinated with archeology and ancient history, these sources are a boon. Enterprising students might follow the continuing excavations online and mine the material for clues to understanding Colossians. Only a few key points directly related can be covered here.

To read Colossians against the backdrop of the Lycus Valley, several intertwined factors stand out. The first is the nature of Colossae, Laodicea, and Hierapolis as hellenized cities in the Roman Empire with local civic elites. Closely related are economic and cultic factors. Prior to Rome, the Lycus Valley had been under Pergamene and Seleucid, that is, Greek, control. Before that, Persians and Phrygians held sway. Colossae was an important town for administrative and military purposes as far back as the Persian period, ca. 550–330 B.C.E. (Cadwallader 2015a, 30). Laodicea and Hierapolis, although located on previously occupied sites, were founded by the Seleucids, one of the empires succeeding Alexander the Great in the 200s B.C.E. (Huttner 2014, 33–36; Şimşek 2017, 3). The chief point for our purposes is that even before control by Rome, Colossae, Hierapolis, and Laodicea underwent hellenization. The cities had civic organizations characteristic of Greek cities including a council and *strategoi*, an important administrative body (Huttner 2014, 33–36). They also had typical features such as agoras, theaters, baths, sanctuaries to various gods, archives, and games. When the Romans took over, they could build on this as they pulled the cities into their political and cultural orbit. The local elites as well as representatives of Rome offered benefactions (gifts) of buildings, gates, games, and the like in exchange for honor and loyalty. This practice is called euergetism. In Colossae, the late first- or early second-century bomos honoring Korymbos for repairing the baths and water channel mentioned in Chapter 1 of this guide is an example of the civic elite honoring one of their own as well as promoting their own status. Still legible are the names of donors along with their fathers and grandfathers and for some great- and even great-great grandfathers (Cadwallader 2011, 172–74; 2012, 110–13). Although there are indications of some non-Greek ancestry, the sixty-six names are almost entirely Greek. Almost all inscriptions in the Lycus Valley are in Greek, indicating donors valued a Hellenistic identity.

Once Rome became the dominant force in the region, the civic elites sought to establish and maintain positive relations with the empire. Laodicea became a site for periodic Roman judicial assizes or court sessions (Kearsley 2011, 131). Coins from Hierapolis and Laodicea have heads of Augustus and later emperors (Huttner 2014, 60). One wealthy Laodicean family, the Antonii, had a pro-Roman history going back to 40 B.C.E. (Thonemann 2011, 205). In the first century, L. Antonius Zeno entered the Roman equestrian order, became a military tribune, and later high priest of Asia (Thonemann 2011, 209–10). His daughter Antonia's grave inscription says she was "best woman, neokoros, and high priestess of Asia, and priestess of . . ., gymnasiarch . . ." (Kearsley 2011, 144). In both Laodicea and Hierapolis, the Roman proconsul dedicated major city gates in 84–85 C.E. with inscriptions in Latin and Greek (Kearsley 2011, 134–36). While the Emperor Domitian donated the Hierapolitan gate, the Laodicean gate was donated by a member of the *familia Caesaris* (the slaves and freed slaves of the emperor who sometimes had key administrative posts), Tiberias Claudius Tryphon. His name appears with the appellation "freedman of the emperor" in the Greek inscriptions on both sides of the gate to highlight his local benefaction, but not in the Latin (Kearsley 2011, 133–37). These are but a few examples of the material presence of local elites and imperial representatives, which reinforced political, social, and economic power for both.

Economically, the Lycus Valley was a major center for textile production and trade internationally, especially for wool and wool garments. People traveled to Laodicea for the Roman regional judicial assizes and cult sites. They also traveled to Hierapolis to visit its famous healing waters/hot springs, travertine terraces formed by minerals in the water, and its Ploutonian, a site dedicated to Pluto, the God of the underworld, and his wife Kore (D'Andria 2017, 212). There poisonous gas emerged from the ground and rites of Cybele, the Great Mother goddess of Anatolia were celebrated (D'Andria 2017, 210–11, 216). Games, including gladiatorial contests, would also have attracted visitors. In Hierapolis, there are many inscriptions dating mostly to the second and third centuries C.E. mentioning many professional associations. These voluntary associations included the purple dyers, dyers, wool-washers, manufacturers, cattle breeders, gardeners [or farmers], coppersmiths, carpet weavers, nail-makers, cutlers, bread-makers, water mill operators, and what likely should be translated as linen weavers (Arnaoutoglou 2016, 281). Agricultural and grazing land surrounded the cities. The members of the associations would have been relatively prosperous, but exactly where they stood economically might vary by occupation and still is a matter of dispute (Harland 2013, 31–33). Some may have included a range of wealth and status and may have included slaves (Harland 2013, 33). The number of freed slaves and slaves in the Lycus Valley is impossible to determine. Estimates of slaves in the Roman Empire vary widely, but an educated guess is about ten percent of the population (Scheidel 2011, 291–92). There is currently much debate about the economic makeup of Pauline assemblies. If, however, many of the Colossians were craft workers, the assembly in Nympha's house might have been held in the living area behind a shop as Oakes suggests for house assemblies in Rome (2012, 85–86). The household code of 3:18–4:1 suggests it may have included slaves and masters, men, women, and children.

The Lycus Valley was home to a wide range of cultic devotion. This included local versions of Greek gods and goddesses such as Zeus, Apollo, Artemis, Dionysos (Dionysus), and Tyche (Cadwallader 2015a, 45–69; Huttner 2014, 43–57). There were also deities with Anatolian origins including Cybele; Men, a lunar and agricultural god; and Lairbenos (Cadwallader 2015a, 45–69; Huttner 2014, 43–57). Deities were associated with periodic games as well as oracles, sacrifices, and healing (Huttner 2014, 43–57). The desire for health and to achieve at least a subsistence level of well-being would have been strong. The size of the necropoleis (cities of the dead/cemeteries) full of reliefs and inscriptions also show a concern for remembrance after death and care for the dead. The well-being of the city would also have been important and cultic activities would have been a regular part of civic life. The Roman emperor cult flourished. The first century included the beginning of the building of temples for the cult in Laodicea and Hierapolis, documented on coins (Huttner 2014, 62).

What of the presence of Jews in the Lycus Valley? To date, no first-century archeological evidence has been found. Commentators, however, cite textual evidence for a Jewish presence. Cicero's defense of Flaccus (governor of Asia) who seized twenty pounds of gold collected from the region in 62 B.C.E. to pay the Jewish temple tax, for example, leads Dunn to estimate a Jewish population of two or three thousand in Colossae (1996, 21–22). Jewish historian Josephus's *Antiquities* 14.241–43 also describes a letter from the Laodiceans ca. 47 B.C.E. informing the provincial proconsul that they understand that the Jews are allowed to keep the Sabbath and follow their rituals (Huttner 2014, 72–74).

In the second to fourth century, there are twenty-three grave inscriptions from Hierapolis that mention Jews (Harland 2006, 223–24). Three use terms that suggest a Jewish association (Harland 2006, 224–26). One epitaph from the late second or early third century likely reveals a Jewish family celebrating aspects of Hierapolitan, Jewish, and Roman identity. This family follows local custom leaving funds to the purple-dyers' and carpet-weavers' associations for remembrance ceremonies. These are to be held on the Jewish Passover and Pentecost as well as the Roman New Year (Harland 2006, 228). A first-century inscription from relatively nearby Acmonia also indicates Jewish integration into a Greco-Roman polis. Julia Severa, a high priestess of the imperial cult and *agonothete* (patron, president of games), seems to have donated a building for the synagogue community simply as a benefactor or possibly as a god-fearer (Rajak 2002, 464, 470–73; for the inscription, see Harland 2015).

Reconstruction of the historical context: Internal and external clues

As this brief description of the Lycus Valley shows, the influence of the Roman Empire was strong. The rhetorical analysis of the letter has highlighted how the addressees might have heard many phrases in the context of empire. Some may have heard a challenge to the empire of Rome with a savior superior to the emperor. Christ had defeated spiritual and literal rulers and authorities and was bringing true peace and prosperity through the cross. While the letter does not stress persecution, the picture of Paul in chains and the nailing of Christ to the cross could have emphasized conflict between the empire of Caesar and the empire of God. At the same time, picking up the imagery of empire might have helped hearers to understand the claims the letter made for Christ. Yet, that imagery also reinforced the sort of power dynamics and hierarchy involved. Male and female slaves and free wives, for example, may have heard the household code as accommodation to the empire's hierarchical structure as we will discuss in the next chapter. Recent scholarship suggests that Paul's letters both resist and reinforce imperial values in very complicated ways. To explore further readings of Colossians that take seriously the context of empire, see Keesmaat (2014), Maier (2005, 2011, 2013, 2016), Tinsley (2013), and Walsh and Keesmaat (2004). Several of these works stress the relevance of Colossians for modern readers living in the shadow of empire.

Turning from the imperial context to questions of ethnic-religious identity in the first century, the Lycus Valley located on major trade routes would have had a mix of people with differing ethnic/religious/cultural roots. Given that almost all the inscriptions are in Greek, the civic elite prized a Hellenic identity even as they cultivated Roman ties. The cities were likely home to some Jews. New Testament scholarship in a quest to describe a development from Jewish to Gentile Christianity has focused most on whether Christ followers were Jewish or Gentile (i.e., not Jewish). Most interpreters assume the Colossian Christ followers were predominantly Gentiles. They offer several key verses as evidence. One is 1:12 where God has qualified you (alt. text: us) to share the inheritance of the saints, indicating that the recipients were not previously inheritors; that is, they may have been Gentiles (e.g., Barth and Blanke 1994, 187; Moo 2008, 28). Similarly, 1:21 and 3:5–7 might point to a past Gentile life of misdeeds (see Barth and Blanke 1994, 21 and 219; Dunn 1996, 214; Foster 2016, 10; Lohse [1968] 1971, 3, 138; and Moo 2008, 28). Chapter 1:27 where Paul proclaims that God makes known "how great among the Gentiles are the riches of the glory of this mystery, which is Christ in you (1:27, NRSV)" might support a largely Gentile assembly (e.g., Barth and Blanke 1994, 21; Foster 2016, 10; Moo 2008, 28). However, the mystery may be that God has included the Gentiles (e.g., Sumney 2008, 106). Chapter 2:13 makes a firmer case. There the recipients are "dead in transgressions and the uncircumcision of the flesh" before baptism. If flesh is taken literally, this would rule out observant, male Jews (e.g., Dunn 1996, 29, 155; Lincoln 2000, 625; Lohse [1968] 1971, 3). Despite arguing for the predominance of Gentiles, many scholars imagine some Jewish members of the assembly, relying on arguments for the presence of Jews in the Lycus Valley as well as the "where there is not Greek and Jew, circumcision and uncircumcision" phrases of 3:11 (e.g., Dunn 1996, 29). The presence of Jews in Colossae and the assembly is necessary for some reconstructions of the ascetics the letter opposes.

Historical reconstructions of the philosophy: The ascetics/visionaries of 2:6–23

As we have noted, most recent interpreters see the central exigence or problem of Colossians as a philosophy that the letter warns might take the addressees captive. The letter uses this philosophy to construct an alternative identity via contrast. But, who might the individuals or groups advocating the philosophy have been in the first century? In overhearing the conversation between the letter's sender and addressees, how do we—can we—reconstruct who the sender was warning against? An apt metaphor for the Colossian philosophy is a puzzle (Barclay [1997] 2004, 51–54; DeMaris 1994, 5). Historical critics love a puzzle and are keen to put together the pieces spread out in 2:6–23 to form a portrait of the opposition. Key pieces we have already identified include (1) asceticism and diet; (2) observance of festivals, new moons, or Sabbaths; (3) visions; (4) worship of angels; and (5) elements of the cosmos.

Despite these explicit pieces, solving the puzzle to everyone's satisfaction is elusive. In 1973, J. J. Gunther listed forty-four solutions (1973, 3–4), an often-cited statistic (e.g., DeMaris 1994, 18; Ehrman 2013, 179; Foster 2016, 106; T. Martin 1996, 11; Talbert 2007, 207). Solutions continue to multiply. We will review briefly several types of currently influential solutions. These include mystery cult, forms of Judaism, philosophical traditions, and syncretism. All use external data to provide additional pieces of the puzzle. For discussion of more reconstructions, see Francis and Meeks (1973), Dunn (1996), Barclay ([1997] 2004, 39–48), DeMaris (1994, 18–40), and Talbert (2007, 207–9).

Mystery cult: Entering in

In the late nineteenth and early twentieth centuries, there was increasing European interest in Mediterranean archeology and comparative religion. One of the discoveries on the west coast of Turkey was a set of inscriptions at the Apollo Oracle Sanctuary at Claros (Klaros), very near to Ephesus. Some of these second-century inscriptions contained the term *embateuōn* (to enter in) found in Col 2:18. This struck both the British W. M. Ramsay (1914, orig. essay 1913) and the German Martin Dibelius ([1917] 1973) independently as highly significant. They both argued that when delegates came from various cities to seek the oracle's advice, some were initiated into the "mysteries" of the Apollo cult and entered in as a second stage of initiation (Dibelius [1917] 1973, 86–87; Ramsay 1914, 288). Ramsay thought this meant that "they performed an act called ἐμβατεύων, symbolizing that they had entered on a new life" (1914, 290). Ramsay added information from other sites and texts to fill out what might have occurred. Dibelius employed an extensive analysis of Apuleius's account of Isis initiation. The Isis cult was an Egyptian goddess cult popular throughout the Mediterranean. With this background, both read *embateuōn* as a technical term that Paul uses to argue against a mystery cult. Ramsay argues that Paul opposes a converted initiate, who now teaches an ascetic, mystic, and wisdom-oriented Christianity (1914, 300–301). Both Paul and the mystery teacher taught a way of escaping slavery to powers intermediate between God and humans: the demonic archons (rulers), angels, elemental powers of the air and heavens (Ramsay 1914, 302). Siding with Paul, Ramsay argued that Paul's approach was spiritual, but the mystery teacher's was "prescribed ritual," "external and non-spiritual" (1914, 304). Colossians 2:8–19, therefore, put the kibosh on any attempt to argue that Paul was influenced by "mystery religions" (1914, 303–304), a view in vogue at the time. Ramsay preserves Paul's uniqueness while recognizing a certain appeal to mystery religion and philosophy. There is also a flavor of Protestant disdain for ritual as well as a Western view of the exotic "Orient" mixed in. Ramsay cites approvingly Currie Martin who describes the people of Phrygia as enamored of "heathen superstition," taking delight in "excitement and mystery" (Ramsay 1914, 299).

Like Ramsay, Dibelius identifies the angels with the elements of the cosmos. However, he thinks that there was a pre-Christian gnostic cult associated with asceticism that venerated them ([1917] 1973, 82, 90). (At the time, scholars thought there was a dualistic religion that promised liberation to divine sparks trapped in physical bodies through special knowledge [*gnosis*; Mirecki 2000].) What happened in Colossae, Dibelius thinks, is that members of the assembly joined the mystery cult as a sort of "double insurance" against Fate ([1917] 1973, 90). He sees this syncretism as an example of the birth of Christian Gnosticism ([1917] 1973, 91). Like Ramsay, he separates Paul's views from "cultus," that is, ritual, but these were joined with cultic actions in Christian Gnosticism (1917] 1973, 96–97). Dibelius also argues for the superiority of exclusivist Christianity over "mysteries, gnosis, and syncretistic prophets" ([1917] 1973, 101).

Both Ramsay and Dibelius honed in on *embateuōn* (entering in) as the key to unlock what Paul argued against—finding mystery religion behind the door—and in Dibelius's case, Gnosticism as well. Subsequent scholars were often impressed (e.g., Lohse [1968] 1971, and Arnold [1996] 2000, who adds a stronger Jewish influence to the mix). Discovering the term in inscriptions was understandably exciting, albeit second and not first-century inscriptions. Ramsay also knew that delegations from Laodicea came to Claros (Ramsay 1914, 288). The scholarly discussion of mystery religions at the time was also significant. Today, however, scholars do not see all "mystery religions" as essentially similar (Gordon 1996). There is also more skepticism of overbroad and vague categories such as mysticism and Gnosticism, especially since the discoveries at Nag Hammadi (Williams 1996). Above all, the creation of a model based on a single word seems suspect. "Entering in" appears in many other contexts besides initiation (DeMaris 1994, 84; Francis 1973b). It may even refer to entering in to an underground chamber to await the oracle after initiation, something Dibelius rejected ([1917] 1973, 86–87; cf. Fox 1988, 173–76). References to festivals, new moons, and Sabbaths and circumcision as well as angels, asceticism, and wisdom in Jewish traditions are ignored or downplayed. Connections to Jewish tradition are, however, taken up in other reconstructions.

Judaism: The synagogue across the street and worship with angels

While Ramsay, Dibelius, Lohse, and others see the teaching and practices opposed in Colossians as largely of Gentile origin, many others find their roots in Judaism. One example of this is the "synagogue across the street" approach of Bevere (2003), Dunn (1996, 23–35), and Wright ([1986] 2015, 25–33). This approach holds that local Judaism—"the synagogue across the street"—presents an attractive alternative to the Colossians (I borrow the phrase from Donahue 1988, 85). Dunn points to circumcision, food and purity laws, and festivals, new moons, and Sabbaths as marks of Judaism (1996, 34). Further, worship of angels fits well in mystical and apocalyptic Judaism where one can "enter in" heavenly worship with the angels as Francis (1973a) suggests (Dunn 1996, 180–81; Wright [1986] 2015, 28). The likely first-century Jewish presence in the Lycus Valley lends support. Similarly, later external evidence shows that Christ believers continued to engage in Jewish practice for quite some time. For example, Chrysostom warned about "attending synagogue on Saturday and church on Sunday" and the fourth-century Council of Laodicea forbid the observance of Jewish feasts and the Sabbath (Dunn 1996, 29; see also Wright [1986] 2015, 30]. Given that Dunn, Wright, and Bevere (a Dunn student) belong to the "New Perspective on Paul" school of interpretation, their views are not surprising. Although an umbrella term that covers differences, essentially the New Perspective sees first-century Judaism as a covenant community marked from its Gentile neighbors by lived expressions of belonging such as Sabbath observance, food laws, and circumcision, not a legalistic religion of works righteousness. This explains why Dunn, for example, does not see the philosophy as heresy and why he stresses that Paul and the synagogue had much in common (1996, 35).

The synagogue across the street approach relies on the work of Francis (1973a and 1973b). Francis argues that worship of angels is a subjective genitive referring to the angels' heavenly worship of God. He draws examples from extracanonical Jewish literature such as the Ascension of Isaiah, Philo, and Qumran. *Embateuōn* means entering the heavens in a vision rather than mystery initiation. The proponents of the philosophy practice asceticism to induce visions in which they enter and join in angelic worship. A difference from the synagogue across the street view, however, is that the ascetic visionaries in Colossians are members of the assembly rather than outsiders. For Francis, "writer, readers, and errorists" all presuppose "the pre-eminence of Christ over all powers" (1973a, 183). But, a difference between the writer and the visionaries was that the latter used Christ as a pattern to be imitated to gain redemption rather than trusting in the sufficiency of Christ's actions (1973a, 184). Thus, Francis reproduces the rhetoric of the letter that creates opposing positions via contrast.

Many have followed Francis's approach (e.g., Kittredge and Columbo 2017; Sumney 2005b and 2008). Others are not convinced. Arnold, for example, argues that the term worship followed by a god or other object of worship in the subjective genitive is never found in Greek literature as Francis's thesis requires ([1996] 2015, 91–92). In support of Francis, further evidence of ascetic-mystical piety in Jewish traditions continues to mount (e.g., Sappington 1991; I. Smith 2006). Porous boundaries between Gentile Christ followers and Jews (Christ following or not) in Asia Minor also lend support as do the friendly relations of Jews and Gentiles shown by Julia Severa's synagogue benefaction and the Hierapolitan family celebrating Jewish and Roman festivals. The letter may stress that Gentiles can become part of God's people only through the spiritual circumcision of baptism into Christ and no other practices should be adopted. The opponents might have thought otherwise (cf. Hayes 2017). There is, however, some danger of anti-Judaism if circumcision and observance of the Sabbath are seen as outward, material markers of a Jewish ethnocentrism overcome by a spiritual Christian universalism (Horrell 2015, 135).

Philosophy plus

If interest in Jewish thought and practice has had an impact in reconstructing the philosophy Colossians opposes, so too has scholarly interest in Hellenistic philosophy. We have already seen that Schweizer interpreted the elements of the cosmos as earth, water, air, and fire (1988, 455). He pointed to texts in which earth, water, air, and fire were in disharmony and could tie souls to the world after death without ascetic practices, something the Colossians might fear (Schweizer 1982, 130–32; 1988, 467). He found a first-century B.C.E. Pythagorean text that embodied these ideas and matched up well with the features of the Colossian philosophy (Schweizer 1982, 132–33). Thus, the opposition in Colossians was a Jewish Pythagoreanism that may "have included some kind of mystery rite" (Schweizer 1982, 133).

Others tie the opposition to Middle Platonism. DeMaris argues that the opponents are syncretists who draw on popular Middle Platonism as well as Jewish and Christian beliefs (1994). Van Kooten understands the Colossian philosophy as a form of Middle Platonism "concerned with the elements of the cosmos (*Col* 2.8), dietary regulations and calendars (2.16–17), the worshipping of angels and demons as well as with the cosmological experiences in the initiations into the mysteries (2:18)" (2003, 143).

Finally, T. W. Martin argues that popular Cynic philosophers are the opponents. They have visited the assembly and critique it (1996). Traits of the opponents in 2:22–23, Martin holds, are unique traits of the Cynics including "extreme asceticism in regard to non-durable consumer goods and a conception of humility focused upon the body rather than honor to others" (1996, 104). The Cynics criticize the Colossians for celebration of the Lord's Supper and Jewish calendrical observances. The worship of angels refers to human messengers like Paul and Epaphras rather than heavenly messengers (1996, 158–60). Normatively, Martin concludes that the letter's rhetoric succeeds in that it "responds to the culture-rejecting ethic of Cynic Philosophy with a culture-affirming ethic that seeks, nevertheless, to Christianize culture" (1996, 206). Martin's reconstruction is strikingly original because it assigns characteristics usually assigned to the opposition to the Colossian assembly. Asceticism and bodily humility, however, are not unique to Cynicism.

While Martin's reconstruction is the most surprising, these portraits are helpful because they draw attention to aspects of the thought world that other solutions ignore or downplay. They suggest how Christian readers steeped in these philosophical traditions might have interpreted Colossians. However, as the philosophy plus Judaism and Christianity solutions emphasize, it is extremely difficult to find a single source solution that matches up with all the features found in 2:6–23, let alone the entire letter. It is hard to jam all the puzzle pieces into a single frame. This is why many interpreters advocate syncretism, a blending of traditions.

Syncretism

A syncretistic solution to the puzzle has the advantage of accounting for features that emerge from a varied Greco-Roman context where we know there was a great deal of creative cultural mixing. Scholars combine various features of Hellenistic Jewish and Gentile thought and practice to reconstruct the other side of the Colossian conversation. Lincoln, for example, advocates a Hellenistic Jewish syncretism (2000, 567–68). Hooker argues that Paul is not combatting opposing teachers, but rather warns recent converts against adapting ideas and practices of Jewish and Gentile neighbors in a sort of home-grown syncretism (1973). One of the most discussed syncretistic reconstructions is that of Arnold (2012 and [1996] 2015).

Arnold picks up on the earlier work of Ramsay and Dibelius. He treats "entering in" as a technical term for initiation into the mysteries, although he rejects Dibelius's focus on Gnosticism. Relying on an extensive study of Hellenistic Jewish and Gentile folk religion and magical practices, Arnold argues that worship of angels means venerating and invoking them for protection against evil powers including the elements of the cosmos ([1996] 2015, 101, 193–94). He concludes that the philosophy "represents a combination of Phrygian folk belief, local folk Judaism, and Christianity" ([1996] 2015, 243).

Many commentators have found part or all of Arnold's case to be persuasive (e.g., MacDonald 2000, 119–20; Moo 2008, 59). Some critics, however, suggest that Arnold downplays the Jewish background of the philosophy (e.g., Dunn 1996, 33). Arnold responded in a 2012 article, defending his view and stressing the Jewish background. He argues that Jewish "shamanic" healing/ritual/magic is key to understanding the Colossian philosophy. Arnold also argues that his reconstruction is relevant for modern Christians experiencing what he calls "spiritual attack" especially in the Two-Thirds world (non-Western world) (2012, 25–26). Christ alone is sufficient to handle any evil forces; no other beliefs or practices are necessary (2012, 25–26). While one might raise questions about inculturation and globalization (e.g., see Antonio 2006), this application does point out again how interpreters' historical reconstructions relate to contemporary concerns.

Returning to Arnold's reconstruction, Sumney appreciates Arnold's extensive research, but finds his methods problematic. He criticizes the use of broad parallels and a few similar terms to fill in the blank spaces in the puzzle (2005b, 54–57). The same term or phrase can have different meanings in different contexts. Angels and "entering in," for example, appear in all sorts of background materials and their context in the letter should be determinative (Sumney 2005b, 54–57). Sumney's criticism applies to any solution that connects the letter with a reconstructed outside individual or group. Historians play a sophisticated version of "Three of these things belong together—Three of these things are kind of the same" game, familiar to many from *Sesame Street*. Historians' perspectives and interests will inevitably shape the selection and arrangement of available data (cf. *Ancient Jew Review* 2017). At the same time, not just anything goes. They submit their accounts to the scholarly community and sometimes a larger community for critique and revision.

Responding to the multiplicity of reconstructions

How do interpreters respond to the many differing solutions to the puzzle of the Colossian philosophy? One response is to keep at it, refining, combining, and looking for new data. Another is to develop a picture that includes a range of probable to possible characteristics taking into account the rhetoric of the letter and a general picture of first-century Asia Minor (e.g., Barclay [1997] 2004, 52–54; Moo 2008, 50–60). Since the rhetoric of the letter constructs a more extensive account of the faith and life that it advocates in contrast, and since there is general agreement about an outline of the philosophy, this may be sufficient for interpreting the letter.

Another response to the multiplicity of reconstructions picks up on how the letter's rhetoric succeeds in persuading scholars that the faith and life it advocates are superior to the teachings and practices it opposes as we have noted. This is not surprising when we consider that Colossians is part of the Christian canon and many scholars are Christians. Christians reading over the shoulders of the implied audience listen to what the letter might have to say today. They may differ in the degree to which reconstructing a first-century meaning is possible or required for modern application. Moo, for example, thinks that a general understanding that Colossians opposes a teaching that "questions the sufficiency of Christ" allows for application of Colossians to "a wide variety of historical and contemporary teachings" (2008, 60). Kittredge and Columbo, stressing that reconstructions are always probable, urge an exploration of how differing reconstructions of the opponents might contribute to modern theological reflection. The position of the opponents can be valuable because it calls forth an emphasis on Christ and the "efficacy of baptism" (2017, 173). It may also represent other valuable voices in the assembly alongside that of the writer. Women and others marginalized by empire might have found in the Colossian hymn and baptism a liberating word. Life in Christ and asceticism might have led women to visionary experiences and to withdraw from sexual relations in marriage, leading to the introduction of the household code (Kittredge and Columbo 2017, 173–74). Reading in between the lines of the letter to find points of agreement and points of debate may encourage theological reflection about how differing standpoints lead to differing responses within the assembly held together by Christ today (Kittredge and Columbo 2017, 174–77).

We will turn to the household code in Chapter 3. Before you read it, you may want to reflect on the James Baldwin letter with which this chapter opened as well as on Colossians. What role do you think historical reconstruction should play in interpretation? How much detail is needed? How important is understanding the rhetoric and structure of a letter? Was your initial understanding of Colossians affirmed or did it change in some ways as you read about how others have approached the letter?

3

The Household Code, Ethics, and Interpretation

Exercise One—Household Codes

Scholars often label Col 3:18–4:1 as belonging to a "household code" form that appears also in Eph 5:21–6:9 and 1 Pet 2:18–3:7. What elements do these passages have in common? How do they differ?

Exercise Two—Lord/Master

Scholars sometimes describe Col 3:18–4:1 as a "Christianized" code of behavior for the ideal Greco-Roman household consisting of free husbands and wives, parents and children, and slaves. They disagree, however, about the degree of Christianization. To form your own initial judgment, first, strike all the references to the Lord/Master (*kurios*) in 3:18–4:1. Read the passage. Then read it with these references included. What differences do you think the references to Lord/Master make in the meaning of the passage? (See Keesmaat 2014, 568, for the translation and play on words involved.)

Thought experiment—Imagining responses

Imagine that you live in first-century Colossae or Laodicea. You are a free male with a small workshop that produces wool cloaks. You, your wife, son, and a female slave work hard to make a living. You are all members of a Christ assembly. How might you respond to the household code?

Imagine you are a Christ-following slave who nurses your own child and the child of your master and mistress who are active in the Apollo cult. How would you respond?

Imagine you are a Roman freedman running an agricultural estate for your former master. You supervise fifteen slaves. How would you react if you discovered a Christ-following slave scribe copying the letter and you read the household code?

Exercise Three—Complementarians and Egalitarians

As you probably have guessed, interpretation and application of the household code creates controversy. It was a bone of contention between abolitionists, slaves, and slaveholders in the Americas and elsewhere. It is still controversial today. Along with other household code passages, it plays a significant part in debates between two camps of evangelical Protestants, who both have a high view of Scripture. The complementarians argue that while God values the roles of both men and women, they are different and complementary. Male "headship" governs both family and church. The egalitarians, on the other hand, argue that the household codes teach mutual submission and that God calls men and women to all forms of ministry. If you have access to the internet, explore the arguments and concerns of both groups on the websites of organizations devoted to each. The Council on Biblical Manhood and Womanhood is currently found at https://cbmw. org/ and Christians for Biblical Equality can be found at https://www. cbeinternational.org/.

Introduction

Western academic biblical scholarship on Colossians has focused since the nineteenth century, as we have in Chapters 1 and 2, on questions of authorship and rhetoric including a reconstruction of opponents as well as theological categories such as Christology, ecclesiology, and eschatology. But, in addition to stories about authorship, rhetoric, and opponents, interpreters tell stories of the ethics of Colossians and how they may speak today. In recent years, contemporary ethical concerns have centered on two passages. The first, Col 1:15–20, plays an important role in recent ecotheology and related church pronouncements (e.g., Horrell, Hunt, and Southgate 2010; Sittler 1962). The second and the subject of this chapter, 3:18–4:1, focuses on the relationships of wives and husbands, children and parents, and slaves and masters. Scholars speak of it as a domestic code, household code, or *Haustafel*, which is German for "house table." Martin Luther popularized the term. His 1529 Smaller Catechism includes a Table of Duties including duties of pastors and their hearers, citizens, husbands and wives, children and parents, servants and masters, and others. In Luther Bibles, *Die christliche Haustafel* ("The Christian *Haustafel*") is the subheading for Col 3:18–4:1 and Eph 5:21–6:9 (Mutschler 2013). This chapter explores the Colossian household code with an eye to the ethical concerns it raises. The chapter begins with a brief reminder of the code's immediate rhetorical context. It then explains the roots of the code in an ancient Mediterranean discourse on household management. After this, the chapter surveys recent interpretations of the first-century meaning and function of the Colossian code. It points out some of the implications for modern ethical interpretation. Finally, it asks several tough questions about how a first-century text speaks in later contexts. The reception and application of the code have provoked great controversy, especially in nineteenth-century debates over slavery and contemporary debates about the social roles of men, women, and children. Before we turn to the rhetorical setting of the code, I want to set the stage for the chapter with an anecdote that drives home the impact that interpretations of New Testament household codes can have.

An often-cited anecdote in African American biblical scholarship is theologian Howard Thurman's revealing story about his grandmother

Nancy Ambrose (Powery and Sadler, Jr. 2016, 114; A. Smith 2007, 35; M. Smith 2007, 12). Ambrose, born in slavery, refused to have Thurman read scriptural passages to her from Paul except rarely the love chapter of 1 Cor 13. When he asked her why, she replied:

> "During the days of slavery," she said, "the master's minister would occasionally hold services for the slaves. Old man McGhee was so mean that he would not let a Negro minister preach to his slaves. Always the white minister used as his text something from Paul. At least three or four times a year he used as a text: 'Slaves, be obedient to them that are your masters . . ., as unto Christ.' Then he would go on to show how it was God's will that we were slaves and how, if we were good and happy slaves, God would bless us. I promised my Maker that if I ever learned to read and if freedom ever came, I would not read that part of the Bible." (Thurman [1949] 1976, 30–31).

As Emerson B. Powery and Rodney S. Sadler, Jr., point out, slaves in the United States often faced white preachers who urged them to submission and obedience with the words of Col 3:22 or its parallel in Eph 6:5–6. (2016, 136). For example, Harriet Jacobs in her autobiography recounts a Rev. Pike accusing slaves of being "eye-servants behind your master's back" as well as idlers and liars and sneaking around to buy rum or stopping to chat on street corners (Jacobs qtd. in Powery and Sadler Jr. 2016, 122). Given these accounts, it is not surprising that Colossians also figured in standard nineteenth-century defenses of slavery in the United States, both north and south (Harrill 2010, 165–92; C. J. Martin 1991, 213–218; Meeks 1996; Noll 2006, 40–45). Today most readers find the use of New Testament household codes including Col 3:18–4:1 to justify slavery appalling. Yet, as proslavery interpreters pointed out, these codes do not—at least directly—challenge slavery as an institution. Similarly, the codes may reinforce the subjection of wives and children to a father, husband, and master in ways that today we find disturbing. As interpreters seek to understand the meaning of the Colossian code in the context of the letter and in the first century, questions about how a first-century text speaks in later contexts hover in the background.

Immediate context in the letter

After the section of the letter arguing against the teaching and practices of the ascetics and for the teachings and life in Christ the Colossians had received, ethical exhortation (parenesis) follows in 3:1–4:6. The letter develops an alternative lifestyle. A former life of vices is stripped off and a new life of virtue is put on. The baptismal formula of 3:11 announces a new community "where there is not Greek and Jew, circumcision and uncircumcision, barbarian, Scythian, slave, free, but Christ is all and in all." As we discussed in the previous chapter, there is debate about whether these ethnic, geographic, cultic, and social distinctions are destroyed, preserved within a new unity in Christ, or perhaps included in the universal rule of Christ. Particularly relevant to the household code introduced a few verses later is whether the oneness is spiritual only or changes social relationships. Verses 12–17 call the community to peace, unity, and thanksgiving and the singing of spiritual songs. Chapter 4:2–6 continues these thoughts with a call to prayer and thanksgiving as well as wise conduct and speech toward outsiders. If the household code of 3:18–4:1 were absent, there would be no interruption of the flow of thought from 3:17 to 4:2 (Sumney 2008, 238). That raises the question of whether 3:18–4:1 is a piece of traditional material inserted at this point in the letter (Dunn 1996, 242–43). Further, whether it is or not, what function does it serve?

The topos—Concerning household management

One reason scholars think the household code of Colossians may be a tradition incorporated in the letter is that there are similar codes in Eph 5:21–6:9, 1 Pet 2:18–3:7, and other early Christian literature. Currently, there is a scholarly consensus that these codes reflect a widespread Hellenistic discussion of the *topos* (common rhetorical topic) "on household management (*peri oikonomias*)". There is also agreement that this *topos* has its roots in Aristotle's *Politics* 1.1253b (e.g., Balch 1988, 26; Dunn 1996, 243; MacDonald 2011, 65–66; Sumney 2008, 230). There Aristotle asserts that the state is composed of households, which in turn are composed of masters and slaves, husbands and wives, and fathers and children—the same three relations Colossians discusses. Household management, Aristotle explains, begins with examining the proper form and nature of these relationships (*Pol.* 1.1253b). The slave is a master's property, his living tool (1.1253b–1254a).

While such general agreement often suggests a scholarly consensus ripe for challenge, the connection to Aristotle is not just a modern one.

In the Middle Ages, Aquinas (n.d.) in his *Commentary on the Epistle to the Colossians* links these verses to Aristotle (C. 3. L. 4. Col. 171, 136) as does English cleric John Davenant in the seventeenth century (1832, 151). Aristotle stands at the beginning of a long discussion of the *topos* from the classical period on. Similar discussions of household management appear in various Greco-Roman sources including Jewish sources such as Philo and Josephus (Balch 1988, 27–29). Ties to the organization of the state seen in Aristotle are frequent. The male free householder should rule over his "natural" subordinates for household and state to flourish.

For the elite, the vision with its roots in Aristotle was an ideal if not always fully realized. The household with its male elite head was an economic and political unit. It embraced a larger or smaller number of members depending on wealth. It sometimes included freed slaves who still had responsibilities to their former owners (Harrill 1998, 162). Those in power viewed the well-oiled operation of this unit of society as important to the order and economic productivity of the Roman Empire including the province of Asia Minor, home to Colossae, Laodicea, and Hierapolis. This was particularly important because Rome ruled largely via local civic elites and ties of benefaction. The ideology of the empire held that harmony and concord in the household led to harmony and concord in the empire and vice versa. Imagery of harmony and virtue in the emperor's family on coins and reliefs encouraged harmony in the household (Maier 2013, 94–99).

Interlocking hierarchies supported one another. A person's place in the hierarchy involved multiple social locations. A freeborn woman, for example, was above male and female slaves, but below her father. At the top of the hierarchical pyramid in the household was the master (*kurios*), husband, and father—the Greco-Roman *paterfamilias*. He was the dominant player in all three relationships. The emperor or *Pater patriae* was the *paterfamilias* writ large (D'Angelo 1992, 623–24). Elisabeth Schüssler Fiorenza describes the pyramid as kyriarchical, based on the Greek words *kurios* (lord/master) and *archein* (to rule) (2007, 153). Kyriarchy, she explains, entails "the domination of the emperor, lord, slave master, husband, the elite freeborn educated and propertied male colonizer who has power over all wo/men and subaltern [colonized, dominated] men" (2007, 158). This hierarchical framework embodied a sliding scale of masculinity with elite males whose rule was justified by their own self-mastery at one end and various "unmen" who should be mastered including females, boys, slaves, and barbarians at the other (Anderson and Moore 2003, 68–69).

While discussion of the topos concerning household management varied somewhat from text to text, the structure of the ideal household was similar. As we have noted, however, not all households matched the ideal form. Where, for example, did a slave fathered by his master fit? What of households with no children or foster children? Of those headed by a widow? There was also room for people to exercise informal agency. A talented, freeborn woman, for example, might have considerable latitude in running household affairs, which often included production of textiles or other items of value.

As to whether Colossians borrowed a preexisting tradition, there is no way to know for sure. As we noted above, that the letter would read smoothly if the code was omitted might suggest the insertion of traditional material. Alternatively, Colossians might be the first or one of the first examples of a Christian adaptation of the topos. It also covers the important sphere of household relationships. This would be important in envisioning the life of the new self and the new community that forms the context for the code. While there are many texts that discuss household management, we currently know of none prior to Colossians that has the same literary structure (Barclay [1997] 2004, 68–70; Talbert 2007, 232). More important than its roots, however, are its meaning, functions, and role in the letter and in later interpretation.

Nature and functions of the Colossian code

While many interpreters argue that the code prescribes a hierarchical household pattern, they differ on the degree to which the pattern has been "Christianized" and the extent to which it is integrated into Colossians. They also differ as to its function. Suggestions range from to render the Christ assembly less threatening to its neighbors and authorities, to bring ordinary life under the lordship of Christ, to soften and support a love-infused patriarchy, to a hidden challenge to imperial kyriarchy. As we will see, the last function is part of a recent trend to read the Colossian code as a mixture of conformity and resistance to existing social structures. The code may very well have had multiple functions. We should also note that Colossians does not specify that the husbands, fathers, and masters are members of the Christ assembly.

Apologetic and reining in: The authorities, the "opponents," the neighbors

Many interpreters see New Testament household codes fulfilling an apologetic (defensive) function. Balch, for example, argues that the purpose of the household code of 1 Peter is to make the community less suspect in the face of Roman suspicions of "foreign" cults and to lessen tensions with unbelieving husbands and masters (1981). James Crouch argues that the Colossian code combats enthusiasm (charismatic practices) that led to slave unrest (1972). There is no sign, however, that slaves were actively rebelling (MacDonald 2000, 163).

Nonetheless, one possible function of the code may be to rein in those whose teaching and practices the letter opposes, as we noted in the previous chapter. This might have had an apologetic function as well as supporting the authority of more conventional leaders. Feminist interpreters such as Bugg (2006), D'Angelo (1992), Kittredge and Columbo (2017), and Schüssler Fiorenza (1983) suggest that free women and male and female slaves might have found spiritual authority and a call to freedom in the Christ hymn of 1:15–20 and the baptismal formula of 3:11 as well as in ascetic practice and visionary worship. If outsiders saw their activities as deviant or saw a challenge to their own authority as husbands, fathers, or masters, this might pose a threat to the community. Colossians 4:4–6 mentioning Paul's imprisonment and conduct toward outsiders might support this view. The introduction of a traditional household ethic as part of what new life in Christ required would put the assembly in harmony with the conventional morality of local civic elites and the larger Roman social order. MacDonald points out that the rituals and practices the opponents may have advocated would have made Christ followers highly visible if they lived in nonbelieving households or even next door to nonbelievers (2000, 166–67). Colossians may call for an invisible "inner asceticism" or self-mastery (MacDonald 2000, 167). Maintaining an identity in Christ without visible markers might have been difficult, but was perhaps necessary (MacDonald 2000, 167).

Unfortunately, from a feminist perspective, the result even when Christians gained power was a blessing of kyriarchal ideology and practice in church and society. However, as Schüssler Fiorenza points out, household codes were "not descriptive, but prescriptive" (2007, 154). Free women and male and female slaves likely continued to play important roles as the reference to the assembly in Nympha's house in Col 4:15 suggests (MacDonald 2010, 76).

They could also exercise informal power in the domestic sphere, especially while the assemblies met there (MacDonald 2000, 168). There was also some wiggle room in the culture. Women were participants in a variety of Greco-Roman cults. Free women and male and female slaves participated together in some cults, even if male elites sometimes viewed this with suspicion (Standhartinger [1999] 2012, 805–6). In Roman Asia Minor, elite women were often benefactors and office holders (Kearsley 2005). Informal power continues today as an avenue for women in churches that limit women's official roles. As we noted in Chapter 2, Christian feminists sometimes argue that recovering other voices in the Colossian assembly along with the voice of the author contributes to contemporary discussion in churches. Listening to multiple voices also raises the question of when wearing the garments of conventional morality is fitting and when new, more dangerous countercultural clothes should be put on.

External conventional morality/internal commitment to the Master

Since the submission of wives, children, and slaves to a master was a Greco-Roman commonplace, interpreters have wondered what difference the seven references to the Lord/Master Christ in Col 3:18–4:1 make. Do we have a "lightly Christianized" version of the commonplace (Dibelius and Greeven 1953, 46, cited in Barclay 2001, 39 n. 6; cf. Meeks 1996, 242)? Or, do the references to the Master/Lord mark a profound difference? Many interpreters argue that while not challenging conventional household morality, the appeal to the ultimate Master is transformative. The function of the code is to hallow everyday life. The external conventional morality of the code is not timeless, but internal obedience to the Master is. Eduard Lohse, James D. G. Dunn, and John M. G. Barclay provide examples of this perspective.

Lohse sees the commands of 3:18–4:1 as entirely consistent with Hellenistic morality. There is, however, "a completely new motivation" for these commands ([1968] 1971, 156). This new motivation subordinates "the entire life, thought and conduct of believers" to the Master ([1968] 1971, 156). Obedience to the Lord determines which commands are binding and requires acting out of love (*agapé*) ([1968] 1971, 156–57). All are one in Christ, but social distinctions are not "transcended or levelled in a frenzy of enthusiasm" ([1968] 1971, 163). Believers act out of love, but in the "circumstances of everyday life" ([1968] 1971, 163). This stance allows Lohse to see the code's specifics and the social order it represents as historically conditioned. The required obedience to the Master, however, must govern each new historical situation.

Dunn makes a similar case. He argues that the main purpose of the code was to show that "household responsibilities" were part and parcel of one's responsibilities to the Lord (1996, 244–45). Christ's lordship played itself out within society's institutions (1996, 245). He agrees with those who see an apologetic function as well. He argues the code demonstrates good citizenship and makes possible "an apologetic and evangelistic impact" (1996, 245). Dunn holds that as a powerless group early Christians chose neither to radically criticize Hellenistic culture or Roman power, nor to withdraw, not to encourage rebellion. Instead, Dunn sees the early Christians as "combining that society's proven wisdom with commitment to its own Lord and the transforming power of the love which he had embodied" (246). In terms of the modern relevance of the code's rules, Dunn, like Lohse, argues that they "are not timeless rules" that apply to modern circumstances (246). The motivation of serving and fearing the Lord, however, remains constant (246). By historicizing, Lohse and Dunn avoid justifying slavery and the subjection of women and children while maintaining a Christian theological relevance for the code. One wonders, however, whether they take seriously enough what the cost of fulfilling a societal role might have been or indeed might be today for those on the bottom. For example, convention allowed masters to use female and male slaves including children as sexual outlets (Glancy [2002] 2006, 143–44). Patriarchy softened by love is still patriarchy (C. J. Martin 1991, 210). Barclay takes account of the costs, although he does not eliminate them. He also works hard to show how the code is integrated into the letter.

Barclay notes that the household code at first glance seems at odds with the Christocentric focus of Colossians, conflicts with what we see today as Christian values, and has caused incalculable damage to those harmed by its later applications (2001, 39–40). Nevertheless, it is highly Christocentric, well-integrated into the letter, and remains theologically significant. Barclay holds that the code with its many references to the Lord/Master puts everyday responsibilities under the universal "Lordship of Christ" (2001, 44, 47). The code confirms the lordship of Christ celebrated in the Christ hymn and throughout the letter because performing the prescribed duties ultimately serves the Master (2001, 43). The believer is transferred into a new realm, a new life, that gives every action a deep religious meaning (2001, 45–46). This is not merely a matter of motivation, but a matter of "a new identity"

(2001, 45). Colossians represents, he asserts, not a "social revolution," but rather a "cognitive revolution" where all of life is brought under the lordship of Christ and "internally 'Christianized'" (51–52).

To his credit, Barclay recognizes that the code has "an ambiguous legacy" in that it can lead to an indifference to social change, can make terrible situations "endurable—much to the master's relief," and "comes extremely close to sanctioning the present hierarchical structures" as a high Christian standard (2001, 48–49). He also avoids several "false trails" (2001, 40–41). The first is to find a special significance to both sides of each pair in the code being given rights and duties. He notes that the sides remain "stubbornly *unequal*" (2001, 40–41). The second false trail is to highlight that subordinates as well as dominant parties are addressed, supposedly unique to early Christian contexts. He notes subordinates are addressed as moral agents "routinely" elsewhere (2001, 41). Barclay's conclusion is that the code "is neither inherently radical nor straightforwardly conservative" (2001, 51). It is an example of German theologian Ernst Troelstch's category of "Christian patriarchalism," a combination of the progressive and the conventional (2001, 51). Barclay writes, "If it has no *principled* commitment to the patriarchal conditions of the household in antiquity (they are only the conditions *in which* one serves the Lord), it also presents no *principled* opposition to them" (2001, 51, italic in the original). This made and makes serving the Lord possible in whatever roles or cultural circumstances people find themselves and whether that service is visible or not (2001, 51). For Barclay, this has ongoing theological significance.

As with Lohse and Dunn, the external details of the household code are not timeless, but internal commitments are. Christians differ on the proper relationship between Christ and culture as theologian H. R. Niebuhr put it ([1951] 2003). Readers must weigh whether Colossians adopts conventional societal morality and places it under the Master Christ. If they are Christians, they must also weigh whether they subscribe to this model of the relationship between Christ and culture or find other models more in tune with canon, tradition, and experience.

Love patriarchalism

As we have noted, Barclay refers to Troeltsch's concept of "Christian patriarchalism," and Lohse and Dunn point to the importance of love in the Colossian code. Many interpreters, even if they end up rejecting the option, consider that one function of New Testament household codes may have been to soften the hard edges of kyriarchy by calling for the dominant parties to exercise dominion with love (e.g., C. J. Martin 1991, 210). In the 1970s, Gerd Theissen interacting with Troeltsch's earlier ideas coined the term "love patriarchalism" for this phenomenon. In a helpful article, Kari Syreeni explains that Theissen treated "itinerant [wandering] radicalism, love patriarchalism, and gnostic radicalism" as ideal types corresponding to "sect, established church, and spiritualism" that occur throughout Christian history (2003, 397, quoting Theissen 1976, 91). Theissen argued that love patriarchalism's modification of itinerant radicalism enabled Christianity to survive as an institution (Syreeni 2003, 397). Critics see Theissen's view as problematic because it implies patriarchalism was inevitable. It operates with a story either of a fall from grace or that of growth into maturity often seen in the stories of the advent of early Catholicism as we discussed in Chapter 1 (Syreeni 2003, 398–99). Syreeni suggests that if we view love patriarchalism not as a model describing a historical trajectory, but as a description of the ethos of the household codes in Colossians and other deuteropauline letters, the concept is useful (399). Chrysostom (ca. 349–407) provides an example of a later love patriarchal interpretation. In "Homily X," on Col. 3:19, Chrysostom (Oxford trans. 1889) writes:

> And see how in nature also it hath been so ordered, that the one should love, the other obey. For when the party governing loves the governed, then everything stands fast. Love from the governed is not so requisite, as from the governing towards the governed; for from the other obedience is due. For that the woman hath beauty, and the man desire, shows nothing else than that for the sake of love it hath been made so. Do not therefore, because thy wife is subject to thee, act the despot; nor because thy husband loveth thee, be thou puffed up. Let neither the husband's love elate the wife, nor the wife's subjection puff up the husband. For this cause hath He subjected her to thee, that she may be loved the more. For this cause He hath made thee to be loved, O wife, that thou mayest easily bear thy subjection. Fear not in being a subject; for subjection to one that loveth thee hath no hardship. Fear not in loving, for thou hast her yielding. In no other way then could a bond have been. Thou hast then thine authority of necessity, proceeding from nature; maintain also the bond that proceedeth from love, for this alloweth the weaker to be endurable.

In evaluating the codes, Syreeni notes that if love makes the negative aspects of domination easier to bear and voluntary subordination is enjoined, the result serves the interest of those in power (Syreeni 2003, 418–19). He suggests that the household codes leave modern Christians with an ambiguous positive and negative "heritage" (2003, 419).

Hidden challenge

While many interpreters see Colossians adopting conventional Greco-Roman talking points on household management, some interpreters see a hidden challenge to that tradition. We will look at three examples: Angela Standhartinger, Jerry L. Sumney, and the work of Sylvia Keesmaat and Brian Walsh.

Standhartinger, as we have seen in other chapters, tells a story of a heavenly letter with a fictional author and fictional addressees written after Paul's death. Writing from a feminist perspective, she argues that the Colossian code wears one face for outsiders and another for insiders (2000 and [1999] 2012). To outsiders it shows that the assembly honored the hierarchical household model and was not a "threat to a 'peaceful society,'" something that may have been necessary in the light of Paul's execution (2000, 127). To insiders, however, there are several clues to read the code "against the grain," that is, against the dominant tradition (2000, 127). The first is that "slaves are promised an inheritance" in 3:24, something not possible in "Roman and Hellenistic law" (2000, 126–27; [1999] 2012, 806). The second clue is that "Col 3:25 appeals to the ideal of the just tribunal . . . where there is no partiality" (2000, 128; [1999] 2012, 806). The third is that 4:1 tells masters to treat slaves with justice and equality (*isotés*) (2000, 128). One can also translate *isotés* as fairness. Standhartinger, however, appeals to several texts where fairness embodies equality between slave and free. The Hellenistic Jewish philosopher Philo in *Omn. Prob. Lib.* 79, for example, describes the Essenes who denounce slave owners for their unjust violation of "the law of equality (*isotés*)" (2000, 128, quoting Philo; also [1999] 2012: 807). These three clues tell insiders that they are not to follow the household subordination model. Colossians mentions masters only in the household code whereas in the letter as a whole, there is only one Master, Christ (2000, 129). The community members are "fellow servants" (2000, 129). Distinctions "between Jews and Gentiles, foreigners and indigenous, slaves and free persons are abolished" (2000, 129). At least some of the addressees, Standhartinger writes, "'blew the cover off' the table of household duties" ([1999] 2012, 807).

Standhartinger's overall argument has been met with both agreement and skepticism. One of the chief arguments against it is her reading of the phrase "justly and fairly (equally)." J. Albert Harrill criticizes those who take the call to treat slaves justly and fairly and to recognize that masters are subordinated to the Master as evidence that Colossians challenges the ideology of slavery (2010, 85–86). He points to conventional "agricultural handbooks which address slaves directly and remind the local farm master (or *vilicus*; bailiff) of his subordination to a greater lord, the *pater familias*" (2010, 86). This elite slave ideally hands out rewards and punishments to the slaves in his charge justly and fairly (2010, 102–4, 110). In Colossians, "Paul" and other nonhousehold leaders are slave stewards of Christ, the ultimate *paterfamilias*. The local householders are like subordinate slaves (Harrill 2010, 114–15). Harrill and Standhartinger make dueling appeals to the agricultural handbooks and Philo to establish the meaning of justice and fairness (cf. MacDonald 2011, 72).

Jennifer Glancy raises the question of what ancient slaveholders, including Christ-following slaveholders, would have considered just and fair. The sexual use of slaves and the beating of slaves as a form of discipline were accepted practice and not considered immoral ([2002] 2006, 143–44). Glancy also argues that treating slaves justly and fairly did not require manumission ([2002] 2006, 143). Glancy quotes Mary Rose D'Angelo's description of the Colossian slave instructions as embodying slaveholder stereotypes about slaves.: "These counsels reflect ancient conventions about the character of slaves: slaves attempt to ingratiate themselves (3:22–23), to defraud (*adikein*) their masters, and to evade punishment by exploiting their masters' favoritism (v.25)" (D'Angelo 1994, 322; Glancy [2002] 2006, 142). In contrast to Harrill and Glancy, others including Sumney, Keesmaat, and Walsh pick up on Standhartinger's clues including justice and equality and expand on them.

Sumney in his 2008 commentary agrees with Standhartinger's interpretation of the subordinates as heirs in 3:24 and equality in 4:1 (249–50, 253). He also argues that the household code instructions in Colossians "have encoded meanings intended to be understood only by persons in the church" (231). His argument adds to that of Standhartinger. He is even more influenced by New Testament empire studies, a renewed interest in the historical and social world of the Roman Empire that benefits from exciting work that classicists and historians have done in the last forty years (Moore 2011). Sumney argues that the Roman Empire advanced a "metanarrative" or world interpreting story that portrayed the gods' choice of Rome to rule over the world, to bring peace and prosperity (2008, 236). This metanarrative undergirded imperial rule. Pauline Christians, while they did not seek to overthrow Rome, were suspect as a sect made up of nonelite members with "a strong countercultural outlook" (2008, 235). To sustain themselves, they created an opposing metanarrative, a counternarrative that told how Christ defeated the powers that control the world through his death and resurrection. Nonetheless, the powers refuse to accept their defeat. These powers sustain the current cultural and political structures and oppose God and believers. Believers resist the Roman metanarrative by living out of the counternarrative (2008, 235–36).

Related to the concepts of metanarrative and counter-metanarrative, Sumney employs political scientist James C. Scott's concepts of public and hidden transcripts (cf. Scott 1990). Hidden transcripts are hidden forms of expression. They capture the perspectives of the subordinated. Public transcripts embody the views of the dominant (Sumney 2008, 236–37). Subordinates express the hidden transcripts or counter-metanarratives in language acceptable to the oppressors, but that only the subordinates understand. This protects them from retaliation (2008, 236–37). Thus, for Sumney, the household code only appears to advocate the standard household model. The multiple references to Christ in the code, the context in the letter, and the context of the assembly where those at the bottom rungs could experience a reversal of social status shape the code's proper interpretation (2008, 239–40). In terms of the literary context, among the aspects of the letter Sumney stresses are Christ's defeat of "the powers that now control the world," believers' "citizenship in the kingdom of Christ (1:13)," the proclamation of 3:11, and the reference to Nympha in 4:15 (2008, 239). A specific example of Sumney's interpretation is his reading of verses 18–19. The call for wives to submit "as is fitting in the Lord" means something quite different than appears on the surface. If all are one in Christ, "wives should submit, but so should husbands" (2008, 242). Wives might still need to submit outwardly, especially if their husbands are not believers. There is a protective, apologetic function. However, if the husband is a believer, marriage is redefined. Marriage means mutual submission and the husband is not to be embittered by his loss of authority (2008, 242–44). Sumney agrees with Standhartinger that "the various caveats inserted within the code direct us to read it 'against the grain'" (2008, 254). Sylvia C. Keesmaat and Brian J. Walsh also view the code as a hidden challenge.

Keesmaat's 2014 commentary on Colossians in the *Fortress Commentary on the Bible: New Testament* and Walsh and Keesmaat's 2004 *Colossians*

Remixed: Subverting the Empire both take a strong stance that Colossians "was an explosive and subversive tract in the context of the Roman Empire, and it can and ought to function in an analogous way in the imperial realities of our time (Walsh and Keesmaat 2004, 7). In her comments on the household code, Keesmaat stresses many of the same passages Standhartinger and Sumney do (although she advocates Paul as author). She makes a similar case and cites their work. She adds a link between messianic traditions and the Jubilee of Leviticus where debts are forgiven and slaves freed (2014, 568). She also discusses how different community members may have heard the code differently. She notes that masters used slaves as sexual outlets. In contrast to Glancy, however, she suggests that Christian masters would have had to stop this practice and that the letter undermines slavery (2014, 568–69). In "The Text in Contemporary Discussion," she asks how Paul's word might speak to those on the bottom of the modern pyramid. For example, she asks, "how does an abused young man who has to sell his body to live on the streets hear this message of the renewal in Jesus in a way that can possibly be lived in his situation?" (2014, 569). Keesmaat presents her comments in a standard format. In *Colossians Remixed,* however, Walsh and Keesmaat present scholarship on the household code in a nontraditional format.

In an imagined letter to Paul from Onesimus describing the assembly's reaction to hearing Colossians, Walsh and Keesmaat lay out three positions the hearers take and Archippus's explanation of what Paul actually meant. (These are three positions we have already seen in this chapter.) The first group thinks Paul supports the hierarchical household structure Aristotle, Philo, and Josephus discuss as moral and God-given (2004, 203–204). The second group fears that not sticking to the hierarchical social order will mean outsiders see the community as a threat to the social order the empire supports (2004, 204). The third adopts love patriarchalism, saying that Paul preserves the status quo, but is calling for "a kinder, gentler economic and social hierarchy" (2004, 205). Archippus explains that Paul is calling the Colossians to live in a covenant community rooted in the stories of Israel and of Christ. Israel's tradition is an Exodus tradition of forgiveness and freeing slaves, forgiving debts and freeing slaves every seven years, and especially in the Jubilee year when "a complete economic leveling" takes place (2004, 206). Paul teaches that God reconciles all things in Christ and rules over all of life. This is why Paul radically calls for the elimination of distinctions (3:11). He also speaks of slaves receiving the inheritance from the Master Christ, also a tradition of Israel (1:12, 3:24–25; 2004, 207–8). The true Master is Christ. Paul "completely" undercuts the household code categories (2004, 208). The hearers want to know why Paul did not just say this clearly. Utilizing Scott's concept of the hidden transcript, Walsh and Keesmaat have Archippus explain that given the importance of the economic and social hierarchy to the empire and since Paul's letters are read out loud and copied, this would be too dangerous. Paul's advice "appears to uphold the status quo while advising tolerance" (2004, 209). But insiders know he argues against the oppressive empire and calls for freeing slaves (2004, 209). At this point, Nympha pops up to explain that Paul is also talking about the whole household system, the liberation of women and children as well as slaves (2004, 210–11). After this imagined letter and scene, Walsh and Keesmaat apply Colossians' anti-imperial vision to what they see as a modern imperial context. They suggest, for example, that consumers not purchase products produced in factories where workers endure slave-like conditions and that parents teach children to see through "targeted advertising" and to understand the interconnection of animals and their environments (2004, 212–19). Although the suggestions target relatively well-to-do North Americans, that is their intended audience. Walsh and Keesmaat embody a Christian Reformed faith stance with strong commitment to a community that practices social justice.

Standhartinger, Sumney, Keesmaat, and Walsh and Keesmaat all rely on the idea that the code may have one meaning for outsiders and another for insiders. This has the advantage of taking seriously the relationship of the Colossian code to wider discussions of household management, the somewhat precarious situation of the early assemblies in the first century, and possible countercultural elements. It also provides a reading in which there is no conflict with 3:11, "where there is not Greek and Jew, circumcision and uncircumcision, barbarian, Scythian, slave, free." One does not have to posit that Colossians distinguishes between spiritual and social freedom. The references to a new self, to a transference into the kingdom of the beloved son (1:13), to Christ's disarming and triumphing over the rulers and authorities (2:15) all make sense on this reading. However, the borrowing of political metaphors including the metaphors of Christ as head of the body and Christ as ultimate Master mean that hierarchical conceptions still run through the letter. One question is whether the community would fear that the letter could fall into the hands of the authorities (cf. Heilig 2015 for methodological issues). Above all, there is the question of why the transcript remained hidden in so many Christian interpretations in the centuries that followed. A reply might be that although the hidden transcript did not take center stage in interpretation by the dominant, some did advocate it as we see in voices of resistance like that of Nancy Ambrose with which this chapter began. More work needs to be done to recover such voices.

From the perspective of many modern readers, the hidden challenge interpretation of the household code is life-giving. Whether as a classic Western text or as Scripture, Colossians would not support kyriarchy. Abused spouses, for example, would not believe that the Bible requires them to submit to abuse, a misreading even under a love patriarchal interpretation (cf. Mollenkott 2003). Other readers will wonder whether modern concerns for social justice are read into an ancient text. To what extent does the insider/outsider reading do justice to the complexities of the ancient text?

When recent empire studies of the Pauline letters began, interpreters read them as resisting Rome. In a second stage, many readings pointed to elements that adopted and reinforced imperial ideology. Today, interpreters often argue that the letters both resist and support empire. Colossians' adaptation of the topos concerning household management can also be read as both resistant and compliant (e.g., MacDonald 2011, 79–90). More work is possible on this front. So far as I am aware, interpreters have made only limited applications to the Colossian code of the postcolonial theory that Homi Bhabha, Gayatri Chakravorty Spivak, and others developed in the wake of modern colonialism (e.g., MacDonald 2011; Maier 2005; Tinsley 2013). Similarly, more readings of the household codes and their reception from differing cultural perspectives are needed. Clarice J. Martin (1991) and Annie Tinsley (2013) provide instructive examples.

Careful readers may have already noticed that while the wife-husband and slave-master relationships come to the fore in interpretations of the code, the child-parent (father) relation is not highlighted as often. This provides another opportunity. There is room for more application of recent work on childhood in the Roman Empire as well as childhood studies more generally. This is something Margaret MacDonald has championed. A discussion and bibliography are available in MacDonald (2012).

The household code speaks: Hard hermeneutical questions

As we have reviewed recent scholarly interpretations of the nature and function of the Colossian household code, I have made brief comments about how interpreters see this first-century text speaking in later contexts.

As part of the ethical exhortation section of Colossians, the household code was meant to impact behavior. As modern readers, especially Christians, read over the shoulders of the first audience, it continues to speak and impact behavior. I want to leave my readers with two questions. The first is, On what grounds would you judge an interpretation of the code's meaning and function in the first century? The second is, What approach(es) do you think faith communities should take in interpreting the code today?

Before I leave you with those questions, I want to borrow, adapt, and add to several types of responses to the household codes and similar texts that Wayne Meeks identifies in "The 'Haustafeln' and American Slavery: A Hermeneutical Challenge" (1996). After reviewing American pro- and antislavery biblical arguments including those centered on the household codes, Meeks asks what approaches we might use in applying biblical passages like the codes to modern ethical issues to prevent the kinds of mistakes those interpreters made. Harrill has also used these categories in a very helpful account of pro- and antislavery arguments (2010, 165–92). Meeks explains that proslavery arguments held that the New Testament advocated the subjection of women, children, and slaves and a conception of society in which such subjection was necessary (1996, 245). Meeks explores four types of responses to similar arguments: "Immutable principles," "The Golden Age," "The seed growing secretly," and "Moral intuition." He discusses the importance of the canon under his "Golden Age" category. I treat canonical and dialogical responses as an additional category. I explore how the interpretations of the nature and functions of the household code that we have reviewed—apologetic and reining in; external conventional morality/internal commitment to the Master; love patriarchalism; and hidden challenge—relate to these responses.

Immutable principles

One typical response to arguments that the household code requires subjection whether in the nineteenth century, earlier centuries, or today is to identify immutable principles within a culturally relative package. This is essentially the external conventional morality/internal commitment to the Master approach of Lohse, Dunn, and Barclay. That is, the specifics of the household code rules are not timeless. We cannot simply transfer them to a very different culture and time. While the external details of the household code are not timeless, however, internal commitment to the lordship of Christ is. For Christians, this approach provides an unchanging rock on which to build. It focuses on Christ and hallows the everyday. As we have noted, however, it may fail to take seriously the costs to those on the bottom (and even those on the top) as well as lead to acceptance of oppressive structures like slavery.

Additionally, Meeks's criticism of the immutable principles' response is that all biblical texts speak from their own culture, their own place and time. He asks how we separate the wheat from the chaff. How do we discern what is universal and timeless and what is culture-bound? (Meeks 1996, 245–46). Lohse, Dunn, and Barclay might reply that we can separate social from spiritual. But that leaves us with the question of how, whether, and if we can and should separate the two. Lohse, Dunn, and Barclay all treat the relationships in the code as time-bound.

A further question about time-bound and immutable principles arises because interpreters do not always agree about which is which. Some view slavery as a time-bound category while accepting the continuing applicability of the instructions for wives and husbands and children and parents. In 1991, Clarice J. Martin, as we noted in Chapter 1, explained that interpreters sometimes reject the authority of the slave commands in the household codes, but accept the authority of those that call for male headship. She discussed this as an issue that black churches needed to address (219–31). The view that what the codes say about slavery is culturally conditioned, but the rest is timeless is not limited to one tradition, however. Moo, for example, while stressing important strains of equality, writes "Other biblical texts make clear enough that marriage (wives and husbands) and the family (children and fathers) are to endure as long as this world lasts. There is nothing even approaching any such endorsement of slavery, however" (2008, 297).

The Golden Age

Love patriarchalism at least in Theissen's case may lead to the view that an early radical critique falls into a later institutional approach that accepts patriarchy/kyriarchy, even as it modifies it. This is what Meeks labels a Golden Age response. If Colossians is a deuteropauline text, some interpreters, especially Protestants, will see the household codes as a falling away from the "real" Paul into early Catholicism and institutionalization—a fall from an earlier golden age. Some might classify reining in countercultural opponents and hidden challenge interpretations as golden age responses because they identify an early challenge to the status quo. Meeks, in fact, uses Schüssler Fiorenza's *In*

Memory of Her (1983) as an example of a golden age response, something she rejects (1996: 247–49; cf. Schüssler Fiorenza 1999, 147–48). However, both the reining in and hidden challenge interpretations argue that kyriarchal and anti-kyriarchal, imperial and anti-imperial perspectives coexist in Colossians. A difference is how each group reads the rhetoric of the letter. Reining in interpreters read the letter as opposing anti-kyriarchal opponents. Hidden challenge interpreters read Paul or a follower as sending an anti-imperial message to insiders while presenting what appears to be a conventional message to outsiders. This has the advantage for those who hear Colossians as a direct address of arguing that Colossians has always taught that slavery and other forms of subjection are wrong. Meeks sees several problems with golden age responses. If a golden age response rests on a reconstruction of history, it begs the question of whether what comes first is necessarily better. Further, its reconstruction can be challenged (1996, 246–49). Moreover, any historical reconstruction of stages is probable, shaped by modern interests, and subject to change (Meeks 1996, 248). A golden age response may pose problems, as we will see, for persuading those who value the canon as a consistent norm (Meeks 1996, 248–49). Finally, Syreeni, as we have already noted, reminds us that one person's fall is another's growth into maturity (2003, 398–99).

The seed growing secretly

Meeks's seed growing secretly response contrasts with golden age views (1996, 249–50). Instead of a fall from a golden age, a liberating seed grows over time. If we apply this response to the household code of Colossians, the references to Christ as ultimate Master; the call to love, justice, and equality; the addresses to both the dominant and the subordinate; and so forth formed a seed that eventually grew to undermine kyriarchy in general and slavery in particular. Along with this, some might claim that Paul or the fictive author could not take kyriarchy head on and have the church survive (Harrill 2010, 173). The hidden challenge/anti-imperial interpretation, of course, can say that the letter does indeed take on kyriarchy if one has ears to hear and so should modern Christians amidst globalization, sex trafficking, the exploitation of migrant workers, and the like. This, however, leaves us with the question of why the hidden challenge struggled to be heard when Christianity became the dominant religion of the later empire. Did the household management discourse coopt the church? What roles did the church's developing canon play over time?

Canonical and dialogic responses

Adapting and adding to Meeks's categories, it is useful to consider canonical and dialogic responses separately. A canonical approach argues that the context of the codes in the canon should determine their meaning. It has some similarities to the immutable principles response and may disagree with a golden age response. For those who assume that all scripture is consistent with all other parts of scripture, it is a problem to say that one part falls away from a preferred original (Meeks 1996, 248–49). This reference to the assumption of consistency points to the importance of assumptions about Scriptural inspiration, authority, and proper rules for reading. One might take a canon within the canon approach or look for the overall thrust of the canon, as Meeks points out. One might argue that central texts or the overall thrust of the canon reject slavery and other forms of subjection. Nonetheless, interpreters still would need to decide what is central and normative (Meeks 1996, 249). One might appeal to one's interpretive community inspired by the Holy Spirit to avoid individual idiosyncratic judgments and/or turn to the idea of the community as a dialogic community.

Interpreters might view the canon as well as individual texts as sites of ongoing dialog between multiple perspectives. As we noted in Chapter 1, feminist interpreters often affirm the importance of discerning multiple perspectives in Colossians to allow faith communities to engage in ethical reflection on multiple perspectives today. One might also adopt Walter Brueggemann's approach in *Theology of the Old Testament: Testimony, Dispute, Advocacy* (1997). There he looks for testimony and counter-testimony from which to develop a pluralist theology and ethics adequate to the community and its canon. A dialogical response often overlaps with the final category, moral intuition, and interpretation from below.

Moral intuition and interpretation from below

The last response Meeks discusses is "moral intuition," as an appeal to conscience. This was an approach that abolitionists used in arguing against slavery (1996, 250–52). As one can imagine, this is a slippery category. How intuition arises from personal and social experiences and how it might form the basis of a reliable ethic are difficult questions. However, Meeks also suggests a practical approach that I see not so much as an appeal to intuition as an appeal to a moral epistemology or theory of knowledge wedded to compassion. A simple example can illustrate. Imagine an adult over six feet tall and a three-foot tall child. They see the world from different perspectives both because of their height and their age. Tall adults might not recognize immediately that a door handle was too high for a child to reach. But they are perfectly capable of recognizing the difficulty and responding when made aware of the child's perspective (see E. Anderson 2017). Meeks suggests that what was needed in the argument against slavery was an appeal to how free people would feel if they experienced slavery and to hear the voices of the slaves (1996, 252). In developing a communal moral perspective, he suggests, people should listen "to the weaker party in every relationship of power" (1996, 252). Christians, he holds, need "to make sure that among the voices interpreting the tradition are those of the ones who have experienced harm from that tradition" (1996, 253, cf. Schüssler Fiorenza 1999, 147–48). This embodies the love the Bible commands (Meeks 1996, 253). Meeks's call is not unique and is increasingly advocated. One exciting aspect of recent interpretation of the household codes is that interpreters ask how people in various locations in the ancient hierarchy including male and female slaves, free and slave children, and free and slave wives would have heard the codes. Archeologists, historians, and literary critics have been increasingly reconstructing what the perspectives of the subordinate might have been. This work on the past has implications for interpreting the codes in the present.

In reflecting on the importance of interpretation from multiple perspectives including from below, students of ethics may catch hints of other conversations. For example, echoes of Kantian ethics that asks whether one would will a maxim of action to be universal if one were to be in the position of the acted upon as well as the actor and commands that we never treat a rational being merely as a means, as less than human (see Johnson and Cureton 2017). Similarly, some might hear strains of Emmanuel Levinas's claim that the face of the other places a demand on us (see Cohen 1986) or Gloria Anzaldua's call to recognize the multiple perspectives of the mestiza ([1987] 2012). If you are a student studying ethics as well as biblical interpretation, I hope that you will reflect on how these two disciplines intersect.

Conclusion

We now return to the hard hermeneutical questions with which I began this section of the chapter. On what grounds would you judge an interpretation of the household code's meaning and function in the first century? What approach(es) do you think faith communities should take in interpreting the code today? These questions are difficult, but worth wrestling with. They raise broader questions about the roles of authors, texts, readers, and contexts in interpretation. I will touch on these briefly in the Epilogue.

Epilogue

At the end of Chapter 3, I left readers with two hard hermeneutical questions: On what grounds would you judge an interpretation of the household code's meaning and function in the first century? What approach(es) do you think faith communities should take in interpreting the code today? These questions raise broader questions. Does a text have a single authoritative meaning or are multiple meanings possible? Is the meaning stable or should it change over time? For example, do the Colossian code or other elements of the letter only mean what they (likely) meant to the first recipients? Or, should we reinterpret the letter in the light of new circumstances? (This resembles the question of whether one should adopt an originalist or a living constitution approach to the U.S. Constitution.) Finally, what role do you think authors, texts, and readers play? As we saw in Chapter 1, there is much dispute over the authorship of Colossians. Nonetheless, we still might want to argue that whoever the sender was, we should try to fathom the sender's intent. Others will claim that this is impossible. We can access only the text, not a human author. As we saw in Chapter 2, we might argue that we do have access to the text, its rhetorical elements, and the rhetorical situation it creates (or reflects). Therefore, the text should determine interpretation. Still others might point to the role of readers. We saw in Chapter 1 that there was much agreement about the style and theology of the letter, but much disagreement about its authorship. In Chapter 2, we saw that there was considerable agreement about rhetoric and certain characteristics of those the letter opposes, but considerable disagreement about the identity of those "opponents." In Chapter 3, we saw agreement that the household code stems from the ancient topos of household management, but much disagreement about the meaning and function of the code in the first century and today. How do we account for agreements and disagreements? Are the differences due to what different readers and reading communities bring to the text? To the different methods they employ? How do we evaluate differing interpretations? I hope these are questions that stimulate further thought and exploration. If you wish to pursue them further, readable introductions include Anthony C. Thiselton's *Hermeneutics: An Introduction* (2009) and W. Randolph Tate's *Biblical Interpretation: An Integrated Approach* (2011). Books in Fortress Press's *Texts @ Contexts* series and the T&T Clark Study Guide series to which this guide belongs also provide food for thought.

References

Aletti, Jean-Noël (2011), "Rhetoric in the Letters of Paul," in Stephen Westerholm (ed.), *The Blackwell Companion to Paul*, 232–47. Malden, MA: Wiley-Blackwell.

Aletti, Jean-Noël (2012), "The *Dispositio* of Colossians: The Exegetical and Theological Stakes," in *New Approaches for Interpreting the Letters of Saint Paul: Collected Essays, Rhetoric, Soteriology, Christology, and Ecclesiology*, SB 43, 311–28. Translated by Peggy Manning Meyer. Rome: Gregorian and Biblical Press.

Ancient Jew Review, ed. (2017), "SBL 2016 Pauline Epistles Review Panel." Available online http://www.ancientjewreview.com/articles/2017/7/5/sbl-2016-pauline-epistles-review-panel. Accessed July 5–25, 2017.

Anderson, Elizabeth (2017), "Feminist Epistemology and Philosophy of Science," in Edward N. Zalta (ed.), *The Stanford Encyclopedia of Philosophy* (Spring 2017 Edition). Available online https://plato.stanford.edu/archives/spr2017/entries/feminism-epistemology/. Accessed July 26, 2017.

Anderson, Janice Capel and Stephen D. Moore (2003), "Matthew and Masculinity," in Stephen D. Moore and Janice Capel Anderson (eds), *New Testament Masculinities*, SBLSS 45, 67–92. Atlanta, GA: SBL Press.

Antonio, Edward P. (ed.) (2006), *Inculturation and Postcolonial Discourse in African Theology*. New York: Peter Lang.

Anzaldua, Gloria ([1987] 2012), *Borderlands/La Frontera: The New Mestiza*. 25th Anniversary, 4th edn. San Francisco: Aunt Lute Books.

Aquinas, Thomas (n.d.), *Super Epistolam B. Pauli ad Colossenses lectura/Commentary on the Epistle to the Colossians*. Translated by Fabian Larcher, O.P. and HTML formatted by Joseph Kenny, O.P. Available online http://dhspriory.org/thomas/SSColossians.htm#34. Accessed July 22, 2018.

Aristotle (1926), *Rhetoric. Aristotle in 23 Volumes*, Vol. 22. Translated by J. H. Freese. Cambridge: Harvard University Press; London: William Heinemann Ltd. Available online Stable TEXT URI: http://data.perseus.org/texts/urn:cts:greekLit:tlg0086.tlg038.perseus-eng1. Accessed July 22, 2018.

Aristotle (1944), *Aristotle in 23 Volumes*, Vol. 21. Translated by H. Rackham. Cambridge: Harvard University Press; London: William Heinemann Ltd. Available online Stable Text URI: http://data.perseus.org/texts/urn:cts:greekLit:tlg0086.tlg035.perseus-eng1. Accessed July 22, 2018.

Arnaoutoglou, Ilias (2016), "Hierapolis and Its Professional Associations: A Comparative Analysis," in Andrew Wilson and Miko Flohr (eds), *Urban Craftsmen and Traders in the Roman World*, 278–300. Oxford: Oxford University Press.

Arnold, Clinton E. ([1996] 2015), *The Colossian Syncretism: The Interface between Christianity and Folk Belief at Colossae*. Eugene, OR: Wipf and Stock.

Arnold, Clinton E. (2012), "Sceva, Solomon, and Shamanism: The Jewish Roots of the Problem at Colossae," *JETS*, 55(1): 7–26.

Aune, David E. (2003), *The Westminster Dictionary of New Testament and Early Christian Literature and Rhetoric*. Louisville, KY: Westminster John Knox.

Baker, Cynthia M. (2017), *Jew*, Key Words in Jewish Studies 8. New Brunswick, NJ: Rutgers University Press.

Balabanski, Vicki (2015), "Where Is Philemon? The Case for a Logical Fallacy in the Correlation of the Data in Philemon and Colossians 1.1–2; 4.7–18," *JSNT*, 38(2): 131–150.

Balch, David L. (1981), *Let Wives Be Submissive: The Domestic Code in 1 Peter*. Chico, CA: Scholars Press.

Balch, David L. (1988), "Household Codes," in David E. Aune (ed.), *Greco-Roman Literature and the New Testament*, 25–50. Atlanta, GA: Scholars Press.

Baldwin, James (1962), "A Letter to My Nephew," *The Progressive*, January 1. Available online https://progressive.org/magazine/letter-nephew/. Accessed July 22, 2018.

Baldwin, James ([1962] 1993), *The Fire Next Time*. New York: Vintage International.

Barclay, J. M. G. (1987), "Mirror-Reading a Polemical Letter: Galatians as a Test Case," *JSNT*, 31: 73–93.

Barclay, J. M. G. ([1997] 2004) *Colossians and Philemon*. Sheffield, UK: Sheffield Academic Press. Reprint T&T Clark International.

Barclay, J. M. G. (2001), "Ordinary but Different: Colossians and Hidden Moral Identity," *Pauline Churches and Diaspora Jews*, WUNT 275. Tübingen, Germany: Mohr Siebeck.

Barth, Markus and Helmut Blanke (1994), *Colossians: A New Translation with Introduction and Commentary*, AYB 34B. Translated by A. B. Beck. New Haven, CT: Yale University Press.

Bauckham, Richard J. (1975), "Colossians 1:24 Again: The Apocalyptic Motif," *EvQ*, 47(3): 168–170.

Baur, F. C. ([1845] 1875), *Paul, the Apostle of Jesus Christ: His Life and Work, His Epistles and His Doctrine. A Contribution to the Critical History of Primitive Christianity*, Vol. 2, 2d. Edited by E. Zeller and translated by A. Menzies. London: Williams and Norgate.

Baur, F. C. ([1845] 1876), *Paul, the Apostle of Jesus Christ: His Life and Work, His Epistles and His Doctrine. A Contribution to the Critical History of Primitive Christianity*, Vol. 1. Translated and edited by E. Zeller, revised by A. Menzies. London: Williams and Norgate.

Beker. J. C. (1984), *Paul the Apostle: The Triumph of God in Life and Thought*, 1st pbk ed. Philadelphia: Fortress.

Betz, Hans Dieter (1995), "Paul's 'Second Presence' in Colossians," in Torn Forberg and David Hellholm (eds), *Texts and Contexts: Biblical Texts in Their Textual and Situational Contexts: Essays in Honor of Lars Hartman*, 507–518. Oslo, Norway: Scandinavian University Press.

Bevere, Allan R. (2003), *Sharing in the Inheritance: Identity and the Moral Life in Colossians*, JSNTSup 6. Sheffield, UK: Sheffield Academic Press.

Brakke, David (2016), "Early Christian Lies and the Lying Liars Who Wrote Them: Bart Ehrman's *Forgery and Counterforgery*," *JR*, 96(3): 378–390.

Brandt, J. Rasmus, Erika Hagelberg, Gro Bjørnstad, and Sven Ahrens (eds) (2016), *Life and Death in Asia Minor in Hellenistic, Roman and Byzantine Times: Studies in Archaeology and Bioarchaeology.* Oxford: Oxbow Books.

Brock, Bernard L., Robert Lee Scott, and James W. Chesebro (1990), "The Sociological Perspective: Introduction," in Bernard L. Brock, Robert Lee Scott, James W. Chesebro (eds), *Methods of Rhetorical Criticism: A Twentieth-Century Perspective*, 273–302. Detroit, MI: Wayne State University Press.

Brown, Raymond E. (1997), *An Introduction to the New Testament.* ABRL, New York: Doubleday.

Brueggemann, Walter (1997), *Theology of the Old Testament: Testimony, Dispute, Advocacy.* Minneapolis, MN: Fortress.

Buell, Denise Kimber (2014), "Challenges and Strategies for Speaking about Ethnicity in the New Testament and New Testament Studies," *Svensk Exegetisk Årsbok*, 79: 33–51.

Buell, Denise Kimber and Caroline Johnson Hodge (2004), "The Politics of Interpretation: The Rhetoric of Races and Ethnicity in Paul," *JBL*, 123(2): 235–251.

Bugg, Laura E. (2006), "Baptism, Bodies, and Bonds: The Rhetoric of Empire in Colossians," PhD Diss. Cambridge, MA: Harvard University.

Bujard, Walter (1973), *Stilanalytische Untersuchungen zum Kolosserbrief als Beitrag zur Methodik von Sprachvergleichen.* Göttingen, Germany: Vandenhoeck & Ruprecht.

Cadwallader, Alan H. (2011), "Refuting an Axiom of Scholarship on Colossae: Fresh Insights from New and Old Inscriptions," in Alan H. Cadwallader and Michael Trainor (eds), *Colossae in Space and Time: Linking to an Ancient City*, 151–179. Göttingen, Germany: Vandenhoeck & Ruprecht.

Cadwallader, Alan H. (2012), "Honoring the Repairer of the Baths at Colossae," in S. R. Llewelyn and James R. Harrison with E. J. Bridge (eds), *A Review of the Greek and Other Inscriptions and Papyri Published between 1988 and 1992*. New Documents illustrating Early Christianity 10, 110–113. Grand Rapids, MI: William B. Eerdmans.

Cadwallader, Alan H. (2015a), *Fragments of Colossae: Sifting through the Traces*. Hindmarsh, Australia: ATF Press.

Cadwallader, Alan H. (2015b), "Assessing the Potential of Archaeological Discoveries for the Interpretation of New Testament Texts: The Case of a Gladiator Fragment from Colossae and the Letter to the Colossians," in James R. Harrison and L. L. Welborn (eds), *The First Urban Churches 1: Methodological Foundations*, 41–66. Atlanta, GA: SBL Press.

Cadwallader, Alan H. and Michael Trainor (eds) (2011), *Colossae in Space and Time: Linking to an Ancient City*. Göttingen, Germany: Vandenhoeck & Ruprecht.

Calle-Martín, Javier and Antonio Miranda-García (2012), "Stylometry and Authorship Attribution: Introduction to the Special Issue," *English Studies*, 93(3): 251–258.

Campbell, Douglas A. (2014), *Framing Paul: An Epistolary Biography*. Grand Rapids, MI: Eerdmans.

Canavan, Rosemary (2012), *Clothing the Body of Christ at Colossae: A Visual Construction of Identity*, WUNT II/334. Tübingen, Germany: Mohr Siebeck.

Castelli, Elizabeth A. (1991), *Imitating Paul: A Discourse of Power*, Louisville, KY: Westminster John Knox.

Chatman, Seymour (1978), *Story and Discourse: Narrative Structure in Fiction and Film*. Ithaca, NY: Cornell University Press.

Childs, Brevard S. (2008), *The Church's Guide for Reading Paul: The Canonical Shaping of the Pauline Corpus*, Grand Rapids: Eerdmans.

Chrysostom, Saint (1889), "Homily X," *Saint Chrysostom: Homilies on Galatians, Ephesians, Philippians, Colossians, Thessalonians, Timothy, Titus, and Philemon*, NPNF1-13. Oxford translation revised by John A. Broadus and edited by Philip Schaff. Available on googleplay online at https://play.google.com/books/reader?id=p3dPAAAAYAAJ&printsec=frontcover&output=reader&hl=en&pg=GBS.PA304. Also available online at the Christian Classics Ethereal Library http://www.ccel.org/ccel/schaff/npnf113/Page_304.html and http://www.ccel.org/ccel/schaff/npnf113.iv.iv.x.html. Accessed July 22, 2018.

Cohen, Richard A. (ed.) (1986), *Face to Face with Levinas*. Albany, NY: SUNY Press.

Concannon, Cavan (2016), "Paul Is Dead. Long Live Paulinism! Imagining a Future for Pauline Studies," *Ancient Jew Review*, November 1, 2016. Available online http://www.ancientjewreview.com/articles/2016/11/1/

paul-is-dead-long-live-paulinism-imagining-a-future-for-pauline-studies. Accessed July 22, 2018.

Crouch, James E.(1972), *The Origin and Intention of the Colossian Haustafel.* Gottingen, Germany: Vandenhoeck & Ruprecht.

Curry, Andrew (2016), "Rites of the Scythians," *Archeology,* July/August. Available online https://www.archaeology.org/issues/220–1607/features/4560-rites-of-the-scythians. Accessed July 22, 2018.

Dahl, Nils A. (1967), "Paul and the Church at Corinth according to 1 Corinthians 1: 10–4:21," in William R. Farmer, C. F. D. Moule, and Richard R. Niebuhr (eds), *Christian History and Interpretation: Studies Presented to John Knox,* 313–336. London: Cambridge University Press.

Dalton, Krista (2017), "Using Harry Potter to Construct a Canon," *Ancient Jew Review,* August 23, 2017. Available online: http://www.ancientjewreview.com/articles/2017/7/31/using-harry-potter-to-construct-a-canon. Accessed July 22, 2018.

D'Andria, Francesco (2017), "Nature and Cult in the *Ploutonion* of Hierapolis Before and After the Colony," in Celal Şimşek and Francesco D'Andria (eds), *Landscape and History in the Lykos Valley: Laodikeia and Hierapolis in Phrygia,* 207–240. Cambridge: Cambridge Scholars Publishing.

D'Angelo, Mary Rose (1992), "Abba and 'Father': Imperial Theology and the Jesus Traditions," *JBL,* 111(4): 611–630.

D'Angelo, Mary Rose (1994), "Colossians," in Elisabeth Schüssler Fiorenza (ed.), *Searching the Scriptures, Vol. 2: A Feminist Commentary,* 313–324. New York: Crossroad.

Davenant, John (1832). *Exposition of the Epistle of St. Paul to the Colossians. Translated with a Life of the Author and Notes illustrative of the Writers and Authorities Referred to in the Work by Josiah Allport, to which Is Added a Translation of Dissertation de Morte Christi. P. Que Pauli Epistola nm melle dulcior, lacte candidior,* Vol. II. London: Hamilton, Adams; Birmingham, England: Beilby, Knott, and Beilby.

DeMaris, Richard E. (1994), *The Colossian Controversy: Wisdom in Dispute at Colossae,* JSNTSup 9. Sheffield, UK: JSOT.

Dibelius, Martin ([1917] 1973), "The Isis Initiation in Apuleius and Related Initiatory Rites," in Fred O. Francis and Wayne A. Meeks (eds), *Conflict at Colossae: A Problem in the Interpretation of Early Christianity Illustrated by Selected Modern Studies,* SBLSBS 4, 61–121. Missoula, MT: Scholars Press.

Dibelius, Martin and Heinrich Greeven (1953), *An die Kolosser, Epheser, an Philemon,* 3rd edn. Tübingen, Germany: J.C.B. Mohr.

Donahue, John R. (1988), *The Gospel in Parable: Metaphor, Narrative, and Theology in the Synoptic Gospels.* Minneapolis, MN: Fortress.

Drake, Susanna (2013), *Slandering the Jew: Sexuality and Difference in Early Christian Texts.* Philadelphia: University of Pennsylvania Press.

Dunn, James D. G. (1996), *The Epistles to the Colossians and to Philemon*, NIGTC, Grand Rapids, MI: Eerdmans.

Ede, Lisa S. and Andrea A. Lunsford (1992), *Singular Texts/Plural Authors: Perspectives on Collaborative Writing*. Carbondale: Southern Illinois University Press.

Ehrman, Bart D. (2013), *Forgery and Counterforgery: The Use of Literary Deceit in Early Christian Polemics*. New York: Oxford University Press.

Esler, Philip F. (2007), " 'Remember My Fetters': Memorialization of Paul's Imprisonment," in Petri Luomanen, Ilkka Pyysiäinen, and Risto Uro (eds), *Explaining Christian Origins and Early Judaism: Contributions from Cognitive and Social Science*, 231–258. Leiden, the Netherlands: Brill.

Eusebius (1913), *Eusebius Werke*, Vol. 7, Pt.1, Rudolf Helm (ed). Leipzig, Germany: J. C. Hinrichs. Available online https://archive.org/details/p1eusebiuswer07euse. Accessed July 22, 2018.

Fewster, Gregory P. (2014), " 'Can I Have Your Autograph?': On Thinking about Pauline Authorship and Pseudepigraphy," *Bulletin for the Study of Religion*, 43(3): 30–39.

Forster, Michael (2015), "Friedrich Daniel Ernst Schleiermacher," in Edward N. Zalta (ed.), *The Stanford Encyclopedia of Philosophy* (Summer 2015 Edition). Available online https://plato.stanford.edu/archives/sum2015/entries/schleiermacher/. Accessed July 22, 2018.

Foster, Paul (2016), *Colossians*. BNTC, London: Bloomsbury T&T Clark.

Fox, Robin Lane (1988), *Pagans and Christians*. San Francisco: Harper and Row.

Francis, Fred O. (1973a), "Humility and Angelic Worship in Col 2:18," in Fred O. Francis and Wayne A. Meeks (eds), *Conflict at Colossae: A Problem in the Interpretation of Early Christianity Illustrated by Selected Modern Studies*, SBLSBS 4, 163–196. Missoula, MT: Scholars Press.

Francis, Fred O. (1973b), "The Background of EMBATEUEIN (Col 2:18) in Legal Papyri and Oracle Inscriptions," in Fred O. Francis and Wayne A Meeks (eds), *Conflict at Colossae: A Problem in the Interpretation of Early Christianity Illustrated by Selected Modern Studies*, SBLSBS 4, 197–208. Missoula, MT: Scholars Press.

Francis, Fred O. and Wayne A. Meeks (eds) (1973), *Conflict at Colossae: A Problem in the Interpretation of Early Christianity Illustrated by Selected Modern Studies*, SBLSBS 4. Missoula, MT: Scholars Press.

Furnish, Victor P. (1992), "Colossians, Epistle to the," in David N. Freedman (ed.), *ABD*, Vol 1. 1090–1096. New York: Doubleday.

Gabellone, Francesco and Giuseppe Scardozzi (2010), "Reconstruction of the Urban Landscape of an Ancient Metropolis in Asia," 15th International Conference on "Cultural Heritage and New Technologies," *Workshop 15 Proceedings*, Vienna. Available online https://www.academia.edu/14627599/

Reconstruction_of_the_urban_landscape_of_an_ancient_metropolis_
in_Asia_Minor_integration_of_2D_and_3D_technologies_and_
methodologies_in_Hierapolis_of_Phrygia_Turkey_. Accessed July 22, 2018.

Given, Mark D. (2010), "Paul and Rhetoric: A *Sophos* in the Kingdom of
God," in Mark D. Given (ed.), *Paul Unbound*, 173–200. Grand Rapids,
MI: BakerAcademic.

Glancy, Jennifer ([2002] 2006, *Slavery in Early Christianity*. Minneapolis,
MN: Fortress Press.

Gordon, Richard L. (1996), "Mysteries," in S. Hornblower and A. Spawforth
(eds), *The Oxford Classical Dictionary*, 3rd edn, 1017–1018. Oxford: Oxford
University Press.

Grindheim, Sigurd (2013), "A Deutero-Pauline Mystery? Ecclesiology in
Colossians and Ephesians," in Stanley E. Porter and Gregory P. Fewster
(eds), *Paul and Pseudepigraphy*, Pauline Studies, Vol. 8, 173–195. Leiden,
the Netherlands: Brill.

Gunther, J. J. (1973), *St. Paul's Opponents and Their Background: A Study of
Apocalyptic and Jewish Sectarian Teachings*, NovTSupp 35. Leiden, the
Netherlands: Brill.

Gupta, Nijay K. (2012), "Mirror-Reading Moral Issues in Paul's Letters," *JSNT*,
34(4): 361–381.

Gupta, Nijay (2013), "What Is in a Name? The Hermeneutics of Authorship
Analysis Concerning Colossians," *Currents in Biblical Research*,
11(2): 196–217.

Hafemann, S. J. (1998), "Baur, F(erndinand) C(hristian) (1792–1860)," in
Donald K. McKim (ed.), *Historical Handbook of Major Biblical Interpreters*,
285–289. Downers Grove, IL: InterVarsity Press.

Harland, Philip A. (2006), "Acculturation and Identity in the Diaspora: A
Jewish Family and 'Pagan' Guilds at Hierapolis," *JJS*, 57: 222–244.

Harland, Philip A. (2013), *Associations, Synagogues, and
Congregations: Claiming a Place in Ancient Mediterranean Society*, 2nd
edn (with links to inscriptions). Kitchener, ON: P.A. Harland. Available
online http://philipharland.com/associations/associations-synagogues-and-
congregations-home/download-the-book/. Accessed July 22, 2018.

Harland, Philip A. (2015), "[145] Honors by a Judean Synagogue for Julia
Severa and Others (ca. 100 CE) ‖ Akmoneia—Phrygia," in Philip A.
Harland (ed.), *Associations in the Greco-Roman World: An Expanding
Collection of Inscriptions, Papyri, and Other Sources in Translation*.
Available online http://philipharland.com/greco-roman-associations/145-
honors-by-a-judean-synagogue-for-julia-severa-and-others/. Accessed July
22, 2018.

Harrill, J. Albert (1998), *The Manumission of Slaves in Early Christianity*, HUT
32. Tübingen, Germany: Mohr Siebeck.

Harrill, J. Albert (2010), *Slaves in the New Testament: Literary, Social, and Moral Dimensions*. Minneapolis, MN: Fortress.

Hayes, Christine (2017), "How Faith Affects the Incorporation of the Gentiles," *Ancient Jew Review*, July 12, 2017. Available online http://www.ancientjewreview.com/articles/2017/6/8/how-faith-effects-the-incorporation-of-the-gentile. Accessed July 12, 2017.

Heilig, Christoph (2015), *Hidden Criticism? The Methodology and Plausibility of the Search for a Counter-Imperial Subtext in Paul*, WUNT 2. R. 392. Tübingen, Germany: Mohr Siebeck.

Heininger, Bernhard (2012), "The Reception of Paul in the First Century. The Deutero- and Trito-Pauline Letters and the Image of Paul in Acts," in Oda Wischmeyer (ed.), *Paul: Life, Setting, Work, Letters*, 309–338. London: T&T Clark International.

Holmes, David I. (1994), "Authorship Attribution," *Computers and the Humanities*, 28(2): 87–106.

Hooker, Morna (1973), "Were There False Teachers in Colossae?" in Barnabas Linders and Stephen S. Smalley (eds), *Christ and Spirit in the New Testament*, 315–332. Cambridge: Cambridge University Press.

Horrell, David G. (2015), *An Introduction to the Study of Paul*, 3rd edn. London: Bloomsbury.

Horrell, David, Cherryl Hunt, and Christopher Southgate (2010), *Greening Paul: Rereading the Apostle in a Time of Ecological Crisis*. Waco, TX: Baylor University Press.

Huttner, Ulrich (2014), *Early Christianity in the Lycus Valley*. Translated by David Green, AJEC 85 & ECAM 1. Leiden, the Netherlands: Brill, ProQuest Ebook Central.

Johnson, Deirdre (1993), *Edward Stratemeyer and the Stratemeyer Syndicate*. New York: Twayne.

Johnson, James Weldon and J. Rosamond Johnson ([two vols 1925, 1926] 2002), *The Books of the American Negro Spirituals*. Boston: Da Capo Press.

Johnson, Robert and Cureton, Adam (2017), "Kant's Moral Philosophy," in Edward N. Zalta (ed.), *The Stanford Encyclopedia of Philosophy* (Spring 2017 Edition). Available online https://plato.stanford.edu/archives/spr2017/entries/kant-moral/. Accessed July 22, 2018.

Johnson-DeBaufre, Melanie and Laura S. Nasrallah (2011), "Beyond the Heroic Paul: Toward a Feminist and Decolonizing Approach to the Letters of Paul," in Christopher Stanley (ed.), *The Colonized Apostle: Paul through Postcolonial Eye*, 161–174. Minneapolis, MN: Fortress.

Josephus (1987), *The Works of Josephus Complete and Unabridged: New Updated Edition*. Translated by William Whiston. Peabody, MA: Hendrickson.

Juola, Patrick (2006a), "A Prototype for Authorship Attribution Studies," *Literary and Linguistic Computing*, 21(2): 169–178.

Juola, Patrick (2006b), "Authorship Attribution," *Foundations and Trends in Information Retrieval*, 1(3): 233–334.

Juola, Patrick (2012), "Large-Scale Experiments in Authorship Attribution," *English Studies*, 93(3): 275–283.

Juola, Patrick (2013), "How a Computer Program Helped Show J. K. Rowling write [sic] A Cuckoo's Calling: Author of the *Harry Potter* Books Has a Distinct Linguistic Signature," *Scientific American*, August 20, 2013. Available online https://www.scientificamerican.com/article/how-a-computer-program-helped-show-jk-rowling-write-a-cuckoos-calling/. Accessed January 12, 2017.

Käsemann, Ernst (1969), "Paul and Early Catholicism," in *New Testament Questions of Today*, 236–252. Philadelphia: Fortress.

Kearsley, Roselinde A. (2005), "Women and Pubic Life in Imperial Asia Minor: Hellenistic Tradition and Augustan Ideology," *Ancient West and East,* 4(1): 98–121.

Kearsley, Roselinde A. (2011), "Epigraphic Evidence for the Social Impact of Roman Government in Laodicea and Hierapolis," in Alan H. Cadwallader and Michael Trainor (eds), *Colossae in Space and Time: Linking to an Ancient City*, 130–150. Göttingen, Germany: Vandenhoeck & Ruprecht.

Keesmaat, Silvia C. (2014), "Colossians," in David A. Sanchez, Margaret Aymer, Cynthia Briggs Kittredge (eds), *Fortress Commentary on the Bible: New Testament*, 557–572. Minneapolis, MN: Fortress.

Keleny. Christine (2014), *Will the Real Carolyn Keene Please Stand Up*. New Glarus, WI: CK Books Publishing.

Kenny, Anthony (1981), "Some Observations on the Stylometry of the Pauline Epistles," *Actes du Congrès international informatique et sciences humaines,* L.A.S.L.A. 501–512. Liege, Belgium: Université de Liège.

Kenny, Anthony (1986), *A Stylometric Study of the New Testament*. Oxford: Clarendon Press.

Kiley, Mark (1986), *Colossians as Pseudepigraphy*, BibSem, 4. Sheffield, UK: JSOT Press.

Kittredge, Cynthia Briggs (2003), "Rethinking Authorship in the Letters of Paul," in Shelly Matthews, Cynthia Briggs Kittredge, and Melanie Johnson-DeBaufre (eds), *Walk in the Ways of Wisdom: Essays in Honor of Elisabeth Schüssler Fiorenza*, 318–333. New York: Trinity Press International.

Kittredge, Cynthia Briggs and Claire Miller Columbo (2017), "Colossians," in Mary Ann Beavis (ed.), *Philippians, Colossians, Philemon*, Wisdom Commentary 51, 123–200. Collegeville, MN: Liturgical Press.

Klauck, Hans-Josef with the collaboration of Daniel P. Bailey (2006), *Ancient Letters and the New Testament: A Guide to Context and Exegesis*. Waco, TX: Baylor University Press.

Krause, Deborah (2004), *1 Timothy, Readings: A New Biblical Commentary*. London: T&T Clark International.

Krause, Deborah and Timothy K. Beal (2002), "Higher Critics on Late Texts: Reading Biblical Scholarship After the Holocaust," in Tod Linafelt (ed.), *A Shadow of Glory: Reading the New Testament After the Holocaust*, 18–26. New York: Routledge.

Kumsari, Halil, Ömer Aydan, Celal Şimşek, and Francesco D'Andria (2015), "Historical Earthquakes that Damaged Hierapolis and Laodikeia Antique Cities and Their Implications for Earthquake Potential of Denizli Basin in Western Turkey," *Bull Eng Geol Environ*. Berlin/Heidelberg: Springer-Verlag. Online publication, DOI: 10.1007/s10064-015-0791-0.

Lampe, Peter (2010), "Rhetorical Analysis of Pauline Texts—Quo Vadit?," in J. Paul Sampley and Peter Lampe (eds), *Paul and Rhetoric*, 3–24. London: T&T Clark.

Lang, T. J. (2015), "Spectres of the Real Paul and the Prospect of Pauline Scholarship," *Marginalia*, May 14, 2015. Available online https://marginalia.lareviewofbooks.org/spectres-of-the-real-paul-and-the-prospect-of-pauline-scholarship-by-t-j-lang/. Accessed May 2015.

Law, Timothy Michael and Charles Halton (eds) (2014), "Jew and Judean: A Marginalia Forum on Politics and Historiography in the Translation of Ancient Texts," *Marginalia Review of Books*. Los Angeles: Marginalia Review of Books. Available online https://dl.orangedox.com/yTWsrMwDFZF3fqx2kt/Jew%20and%20Judean.pdf. Accessed July 23, 2018.

Ledger, Gerard (1995), "An Exploration of Differences in the Pauline Epistles Using Multivariate Statistical Analysis," *Literary and Linguistic Computing*, 10(2): 85–97.

Leppä, Outi (2003), *The Making of Colossians: A Study on the Formation and Purpose of a Deutero-Pauline Letter*, PFES 86. Helsinki, Finland: Finnish Exegetical Society.

Lincoln, Andrew T. (2000), "The Letter to the Colossians," in Leander E. Keck (ed.), *The New Interpreter's Bible: A Commentary in Twelve Volumes, Volume XI: 2 Corinthians, Galatians, Ephesians, Philippians, Colossians, 1 & 2 Thessalonians, 1 & 2 Timothy, Titus, Philemon*, NIB 11, 551–669. Nashville, TN: Abingdon.

Lohse, Eduard ([1968]1971), *Colossians and Philemon: A Commentary on the Epistles to the Colossians and to Philemon*, Hermeneia. Translated by W. R. Poehlmann and R. J. Karris and edited by Helmut Koester. Philadelphia: Fortress Press.

Love, Harold (2002), *Attributing Authorship: An Introduction*. Cambridge: Cambridge University Press.

MacDonald, Margaret Y. (2000), *Colossians and Ephesians*, SP 17. Collegeville, MN: Liturgical Press.

MacDonald, Margaret Y. (2011), "Beyond Identification of the Topos of Household Management: Reading the Household Codes in Light of Recent

Methodologies and Theoretical Perspectives in the Study of the New Testament," *NTS,* 57(1): 65–90.

MacDonald, Margaret Y. (2012), "Reading the New Testament Household Codes in Light of New Research on Children and Childhood in the Roman World," *Studies in Religion/Sciences Religieuses,* 41(3): 376–387.

Maier, Harry O. (2005), "A Sly Civility: Colossians and Empire," *JSNT,* 27(3): 323–349.

Maier, Harry O. (2011), "Reading Colossians in the Ruins: Roman Imperial Iconography, Moral Transformation, and the Construction of Christian Identity in the Lycus Valley," in Alan H. Cadwallader and Michael Trainor (eds), *Colossae in Space and Time: Linking to an Ancient City,* 212–231. Göttingen, Germany: Vandenhoeck & Ruprecht.

Maier, Harry O. (2013), *Picturing Paul in Empire: Imperial Image, Text and Persuasion in Colossians, Epehsians and the Pastoral Epistles.* London: Bloomsbury T&T Clark.

Maier, Harry O. (2016), "Colossians, Ephesians, and Empire," in Adam Winn (ed.), *An Introduction to Empire in the New Testament,* Resources for Biblical Study Book 84, 189–202. Atlanta, GA: SBL Press.

Malbon, Elizabeth Struthers (2008), "Narrative Criticism: How Does the Story Mean?' in Janice Capel Anderson and Stephen D. Moore (eds), *Mark and Method: New Approaches in Biblical Studies,* 2nd edn, 29–58. Minneapolis, MN: Fortress.

Marguerat, Daniel (2013), "Paul after Paul: A (Hi)story of Reception," in Daniel Marguerat (ed.), *Paul in Acts and in His Letters,* WUNT 31, 1–21. Tübingen, Germany: Mohr Siebeck.

Martin, Clarice J. (1991), "The *Haustafeln* (Household Codes) in African American Biblical Interpretation: 'Free Slaves' and 'Subordinate Women,'" in Cain Hope Felder (ed.), *Stony the Road We Trod: African American Biblical Interpretation,* 206–231. Minneapolis, MN: Fortress.

Martin, Troy W. (1996), *By Philosophy and Empty Deceit: Colossians as Response to a Cynic Critique,* JSNTSup 118. Sheffield, UK: Sheffield Academic Press.

Martin, Troy W. (ed.) (2015), *Genealogies of New Testament Rhetorical Criticism.* Minneapolis, MN: Fortress.

Mayerhoff, Ernst Theodor (1838), *Der Brief an die Colosser: Mit vornehmlicher Berücksichtigung der 3 Pastoralbriefe kritisch geprüft.* Berlin: Hermann Schulze. Available online http://reader.digitale-sammlungen.de/de/fs1/object/display/bsb10411841_00005.html and https://books.google.com/books?id=wHhAAAAAcAAJ&pg=PP5#v=onepage&q&f=false. Accessed July 23, 2018.

Mealand, David L. (1989), "Positional Stylometry Reassessed: Testing a Seven Epistle Theory of Pauline Authorship," *NTS,* 35(2): 266–286.

Mealand, David L. (1995), "The Extent of the Pauline Corpus: A Multivariate Approach," *JSNT*, 59: 61–92.

Meeks, Wayne A. (1996), "The 'Haustafeln' and American Slavery: A Hermeneutical Challenge," in Eugene H. Lovering and Jerry L. Sumney (eds), *Theology and Ethics in Paul and His Interpreters: Essays in Honor of Victor Paul Furnish*, 234–253. Nashville, TN: Abingdon.

Mirecki, Paul (2000), "Gnosticism, Gnosis," in David Noel Freedman, Allen C. Myers, and Astrid B. Beck (eds), *Eerdmans Dictionary of the Bible*, 308–309. Grand Rapids, MI: Eerdmans.

Mitchell, Margaret M. (2002), *The Heavenly Trumpet: John Chrysostom and the Art of Pauline Interpretation*. Louisville, KY: Westminster/John Knox.

Mollenkott, Virgina Ramey (2003), "Emancipative Elements in Ephesians 5:21–33: Why Feminist Scholarship Has (Often) Left Them Unmentioned, and Why They Should Be Emphasized," in Amy-Jill Levine with Marianne Blickenstaff (eds), *A Feminist Companion to the Deutero-Pauline Epistles*, 37–58. Cleveland, OH: Pilgrim Press.

Moo, Douglas J. (2008), *The Letters to the Colossians and Philemon*, The Pillar New Testament Commentary. Grand Rapids, MI: Eerdmans.

Moore, Stephen D. (2011), "Paul After Empire," in Christopher D. Stanley (ed.), *The Colonized Apostle*, 9–23. Minneapolis, MN: Fortress.

Murphy-O'Connor, Jerome (1995), *Paul the Letter Writer*. Collegeville, MN: Liturgical Press.

Mutschler, Bernhard (2013), "Haustafel," *Bibelwissenschaft.de Die Deutsche Bibelgesellschaft*. (September 2013). Available online Permanent Link https://www.bibelwissenschaft.de/de/stichwort/46870/. Accessed July 23, 2018.

Neumann, Kenneth J. (1990), *The Authenticity of the Pauline Epistles in the Light of Stylostatistical Analysis*, SBLDS 120. Atlanta, GA: Scholars Press.

Niebuhr, H. Richard ([1951] 2003), *Christ & Culture*. New York: HarperCollins World.

Noll, Mark A. (2006), *The Civil War as a Theological Crisis*, The Steven and Janice Brose Lectures in the Civil War Era. Chapel Hill: The University of North Carolina Press.

Oakes, Peter S. (2012), "Economic Approaches: Scarce Resources and Interpretive Opportunities," in Joseph A. Marchal (ed.), *Studying Paul's Letters: Contemporary Perspectives and Methods*, 75–92. Minneapolis, MN: Fortress.

O'Brien, Peter T. (1982), *Colossians, Philemon*, WBC 44. Waco, TX: Word Books.

Orosius, Paulus (1964), *Seven Books of History against the Pagans; Fathers of the Church: A New Translation*, Vol. 50. Translated by Roy J. Defferari.

Baltimore, MD: Catholic University of America Press. Available online ProQuest ebrary. Accessed June 16, 2015.

Penner, Todd and Davina C. Lopez (2012), "Rhetorical Approaches: Introducing the Art of Persuasion in Paul and Pauline Studies," in Joseph A. Marchal (ed.), *Studying Paul's Letters: Contemporary Perspectives and Methods*, 33–52. Minneapolis, MN: Fortress.

Pervo, Richard I. (2010), *The Making of Paul: Constructions of the Apostle in Early Christianity*. Minneapolis, MN: Fortress.

Pervo, Richard I. (2015), "Remembering Paul: Ancient and Modern Contests over the Image of the Apostle by Benjamin L. White," *Journal of Early Christian Studies*, 23(2): 330–331.

Porrovechio, Mark J. and Celeste Michelle Condit (2016), *Contemporary Rhetorical Theory, A Reader*, 2nd edn. New York: Guilford Press.

Powery, Emerson B. and Rodney S. Sadler, Jr. (2016), *The Genesis of Liberation: Biblical Interpretation in the Antebellum Narratives of the Enslaved*. Louisville, KY: Westminster John Knox.

Rajak, Tessa (2002), *The Jewish Dialogue with Greece and Rome: Studies in Cultural and Social Interaction*. Leiden, the Netherlands: Brill.

Ramsay, William M. (1914), "The Relation of Paul to the Greek Mysteries," in William M. Ramsay (ed.), *The Teaching of Paul in Terms of the Present Day*, 2nd edn, 283–305. London: Hoddern and Stoughton. Available online Open library edition OL7039974M, https://archive.org/details/teachingofpaulin00ramsuoft. Accessed July 23, 2018.

Rehak, Melanie (2005), *Girl Sleuth: Nancy Drew and the Women Who Created Her*. Orlando, FL: Mariner Books/Harcourt.

Reicke, Bo (1973), "Historical Setting of Colossians," *RevExp*, 70(4): 429–438.

Richards, E. Randolph (2004), *Paul and First-Century Letter Writing: Secretaries, Composition and Collection*. Downers Grove, IL: Intervarsity Press.

Ritti, Tullia (2006), *An Epigraphic Guide to Hierapolis*. Translated by Paul Arthur. Istanbul, Turkey: Ege Yayinlari.

Roetzel, Calvin J. (1999), *Paul: The Man and the Myth*. Minneapolis, MN: Fortress.

Roetzel, Calvin J. (2015), *The Letters of Paul: Conversations in Context*, 6th edn. Louisville, KY: Westminster-John Knox.

Rudman, Joseph (2006), "Authorship Attribution; Statistical and Computational Methods," in E. K. Brown and Anne Anderson (eds), *Encyclopedia of Language and Linguistics*, 611–617. Boston: Elsevier.

Rudman, Joseph (2012), "The State of Non-Traditional Authorship Attribution Studies—2012: Some Problems and Solutions," *English Studies*, 93(3): 259–274.

Sanders, E. P. (1966), "Literary Dependence in Colossians," *JBL*, 85(1): 28–45.

Sanders, E. P. (2005), "Review of Outi Leppä, *The Making of Colossians: A Study in the Formation and Purpose of a Deutero-Pauline Letter*," *Review of Biblical Literature* [http://www.bookreviews.org]

Sappington, Thomas J. (1991), *Revelation and Redemption at Colossae*, JSNTSup 53. Sheffield, UK: JSOT Press.

Scheidel, Walter (2011), "The Roman Slave Supply," in K. Bradley and P. Cartledge (eds), *The Cambridge World History of Slavery, 1: The Ancient Mediterranean World*, 287–310. Cambridge: Cambridge University Press.

Schüssler Fiorenza, Elisabeth (1983), *In Memory of Her: A Feminist Theological Reconstruction of Christian Origins*. New York: Crossroad.

Schüssler Fiorenza, Elisabeth (1999), *Rhetoric and Ethic: The Politics of Biblical Studies*. Minneapolis, MN: Fortress Press.

Schüssler Fiorenza, Elisabeth (2007), *The Power of the Word: Scripture and the Rhetoric of Empire*. Minneapolis, MN: Fortress Press.

Schweizer, Eduard (1982), *The Letter to the Colossians: A Commentary*. Translated by Andrew Chester. Minneapolis, MN: Augsburg.

Schweizer, Eduard (1988) "Slaves of the Elements and Worshipers of Angels: Gal. 4:3,9 and Col. 2:8, 18, 20," *JBL*, 107(3): 455–468.

Scott, James C. (1990), *Domination and the Arts of Resistance: Hidden Transcripts*. New Haven, CT: Yale University Press.

Seesengood. Robert Paul (2010), *Paul: A Brief History*. Malden, MA: Wiley-Blackwell.

Shkul, Minna (2013), "New Identity and Cultural Baggage: Identity and Otherness in Colossians," in J. Brian Tucker and Coleman A. Baker (eds), *T&T Clark Handbook to Social Identity in the New Testament*, 367–387. London: Bloomsbury T&T Clark.

Şimşek, Celal (2017), "Urban Planning of Laodikeia on the Lykos in Light of New Evidence," in Celal Şimşek and Francesco D'Andria (eds), *Landscape and History in the Lykos Valley: Laodikeia and Hierapolis in Phrygia*, 1–52. Cambridge: Cambridge Scholars Publishing.

Şimşek, Celal and Francesco D'Andria (eds) (2017), *Landscape and History in the Lykos Valley: Laodikeia and Hierapolis in Phrygia*. Cambridge: Cambridge Scholars Publishing.

Sittler, Joseph A. (1962), "Called to Unity," *The Ecumenical Review*, 14 (January 1962): 177–187.

Smith, Abraham (2007), "Paul and African American Biblical Interpretation," in Brian K. Blount (ed.), *True to Our Native Land: An African American New Testament Commentary*, 31–42. Minneapolis, MN: Fortress.

Smith, Ian (2006), *Heavenly Perspective: A Study of the Apostle Paul's Response to a Jewish Mystical Movement at Colossae*. LNTS, London: T&T Clark.

Smith, Mitzi J. (2007), "Slavery in the Early Church," in Brian K. Blount
  (ed.), *True to Our Native Land: An African American New Testament
  Commentary*, 11–22. Minneapolis, MN: Fortress.
Standhartinger, Angela ([1999] 2012), "Colossians: The Origins of the Table
  of Household Duties," in Luise Schottroff and Marie-Theres Wacker (eds),
  Feminist Biblical Interpretation: A Compendium, 796–809. Translated by
  Everett R. Kalin. Grand Rapids MI: Eerdmans.
Standhartinger, Angela (2000), "The Origin and Intention of the Household
  Code in Colossians," *JSNT*, 79: 117–130.
Standhartinger, Angela (2004), "Colossians and the Pauline School," *NTS*,
  50(4): 572–593.
Standhartinger, Angela (2010), "Kolosserbrief," *Das Bibellexicon*, WiBiLex.
  Bibelwissenschaft.de, Available online Permanent link to article https://
  www.bibelwissenschaft.de/stichwort/51912/. Accessed July 23, 2018.
Standhartinger, Angela (2011), "Kolossae," *Das Bibellexicon*, WiBiLex.
  Bibelwissenschaft.de. Available online Permanent Link to Article: https://
  www.bibelwissenschaft.de/de/stichwort/51913/. Accessed July 23, 2018.
Stillinger, Jack (1991), *Multiple Authorship and the Myth of Solitary Genius*.
  New York: Oxford University Press. ProQuest ebrary.
Sumney, Jerry L. (2002), "The Argument of Colossians," in Anders Eriksson,
  Thomas H. Olbricht, and Walter Übelacker (eds), *Rhetorical Argumentation
  in Biblical Texts: Essays from the Lund 2000 Conference*, 39–54. Harrisburg,
  PA: Trinity Press International.
Sumney, Jerry L. (2005a), "Review of Outi Leppä, T*he Making of Colossians: A
  Study on the Formation and Purpose of Deutero-Pauline Letter*," *Catholic
  Biblical Quarterly*, 67(4): 717–719. Available online Stable URL: http://www.
  jstor.org/stable/43725620. Accessed July 23, 2018.
Sumney, Jerry L. (2005b), "Studying Paul's Opponents: Advances and
  Challenges," in Stanley E. Porter (ed.), *Paul and His Opponents*, 7–58.
  Leiden, the Netherlands: Brill.
Sumney, Jerry L. (2008), *Colossians: A Commentary*. NTL, Louisville,
  KY: Westminster John Knox.
Syreeni, Kari (2003), "Paul and Love Patriarchalism: Problems and Prospects,"
  In die Skriflig/In Luce Verbi, 37(3): 395–422. Available online DOI: 10.4102/
  ids.v37i3.475. Accessed July 22, 2018.
Tacitus, Cornelius (1942), *Annals*, in Alfred John Church and William Jackson
  Brodribb (trans), *Complete Works of Tacitus, Ann.* 14:27. New York: Random
  House. Edited for Perseus. Available online Work URI http://data.perseus.
  org/texts/urn:cts:latinLit:phi1351.phi005. Accessed July 23, 2018.
Talbert, Charles H. (2007), *Ephesians and Colossians*, Paideia Commentaries
  on the New Testament. Grand Rapids, MI: Baker Academic.

Tate, W. Randolph (2011), *Biblical Interpretation: An Integrated Approach*. Grand Rapids, MI: Baker Academic.

Thatcher, Tom (2008), "Anatomies of the Fourth Gospel: Past, Present, and Future Probes," in Tom Thatcher and Stephen D. Moore (eds), *Anatomies of Narrative Criticism: The Past, Present, and Futures of the Fourth Gospel as Literature*, 1–38. Atlanta, GA: SBL.

Theissen, Gerd (1976), "Itinerant Radicalism: The Tradition of Jesus Sayings from the Perspective of the Sociology of Literature," in Norman Gottwald and Antoinette Clark Wire (eds), *The Bible and Liberation: A Radical Religion Reader*, 84–93. Berkeley, CA: Community for Religious Research and Education.

Thiselton, Anthony C. (2009), *Hermeneutics: An Introduction*. Grand Rapids, MI: Eerdmans.

Thonemann, Peter (2011), *The Maeander Valley: A Historical Geography from Antiquity to Byzantium*. Cambridge: Cambridge University Press.

Thonemann, Peter (2013), "Phrygia: An Anarchist History, 950 BC–AD 100," in P. Thonemann (ed.), *Roman Phrygia: Culture and Society*, 1–40. Cambridge: Cambridge University Press.

Thorne, Jack (2016), *Harry Potter and the Cursed Child, Parts One and Two, Based on an Original New Story by J. K. Rowling, John Tiffany, and Jack Thorne*. New York: Arthur A. Levine Books.

Thurman, Howard ([1949] 1976), *Jesus and the Disinherited*. Boston: Beacon Press.

Tinsley, Annie (2013), *A Postcolonial African American Re-Reading of Colossians*. New York: Palgrave Macmillan.

Trebilco, Paul (2011), "Christians in the Lycus Valley," in Alan H. Cadwallader and Michael Trainor (eds), *Colossae in Space and Time: Linking to an Ancient City*, 180–211. Göttingen, Germany: Vandenhoeck & Ruprecht.

van Kooten, George H. (2003), *Cosmic Christology in Paul and the Pauline School: Colossians and Ephesians in the Context of Graeco-Roman Cosmology, with a New Synopsis of the Greek Text*, 135–146. Tübingen, Germany: Mohr Siebeck.

Walsh, Brian J. and Sylvia C. Keesmaat (2004), *Colossians Remixed: Subverting the Empire*. Downers Grove, IL: InterVarsity Press.

West, Stephanie (2002), "Scythians," in Egbert J. Bakker, Irene J. F. de Jong, and Hans van Wees (eds), *Brill's Companion to Herodotus*, 437–456. Leiden, the Netherlands: Brill.

White, Benjamin L. (2014), *Remembering Paul: Ancient and Modern Contests over the Image of the Apostle*. New York: Oxford University Press.

Wickman, Forrest (2012), "*The Grey Album* Gets Remastered," *Brow Beat—Slate's Culture Blog*, November 28, 2012, 1:05 PM. Available online http://www.slate.com/blogs/browbeat/2012/11/28/

the_grey_album_remastered_download_or_stream_the_unauthorized_
remastering.html. Accessed February 4, 2017.

Williams, Michael A. (1996), *Rethinking "Gnosticism": An Argument for Dismantling a Dubious Category*. Princeton, NJ: Princeton University Press.

Wilson, Robert. McL. (2005), *A Critical and Exegetical Commentary on Colossians and Philemon*. ICC, Edinburgh, Scotland: T&T Clark.

Wire, Antoinette Clark (1990), *The Corinthian Women Prophets: A Reconstruction through Paul's Rhetoric*. Minneapolis, MN: Fortress Press.

Witherington III, Ben (2007), *The Letters to Philemon, the Colossians, and the Ephesians: A Socio-Rhetorical Commentary on the Captivity Epistles*. Grand Rapids, MI: Eerdmans.

Wright, N. T. ([1986] 2015), *Colossians and Philemon*. TNTC, Downers Grove, IL: InterVarsity Press.

Author Index

Scripture Index

Subject Index